Southern Keto Cookbook

100 Traditional High-Fat, Low-Carb Favorite Recipes

Janet Rooks

ISBN-13: 979- 8551387121

DEDICATION

To all who desire to live life to the fullest!

TABLE OF CONTENT

INTRODUCTION

The Southern Cuisine has a unique peculiarity on its own, with an identity normally accustomed to the Chinese, French, Italian, and Mexican cuisines. Basically, Southern Cuisine is as varied and fascinating as the various cultures that birthed it.

A style of cooking as diverse with an interesting cultural history as that of Southern Cuisine has over the years become one of America's favorite and popular ways of cooking.

Customary Southern cooking, which is now and then alluded to as nation cooking, homemade cooking, or soul food, depends majorly on corn, pork, rice, fresh vegetables, chicken, fresh seafood, and neighborhood game.

HISTORY OF THE SOUTHERN CUISINE

Southern Cuisine is a mix of various social influences from all around the World, and every one of these impacts has helped the cuisine become what it is today. Significantly dependent on the neighborhood and imported ingredients, need and judiciousness in spending, Southern Cuisine was conceived from the undying longing to survival by the immigrant who settled down in the Southern region of America.

At the time when the first Europeans relocated to North America, they settled down in the Southern District of America and came along with their very own assortment of seeds and vegetables, sugar, flour, milk, and eggs were among the ingredients that brought, and with time, the South Americans began to integrate the Europeans food into their own diets. In the same way, the West Africans and Scottish came along with a variety of their own grains, vegetables, and ingredients with their own style of cooking, and these were soon incorporated into Southern Cuisine.

African ingredients like black-eyed peas and okra soon became a staple of the Southern eating routine, in addition to the local green staples of collards, kale, turnips, peaches, peanuts, pecans, walnuts, and mustard.

Southern Cuisine is unique because of the individuals who prepare it and the culture that keeps on protecting it. The foundations of the cuisine run solid from its multifaceted, its blend of notable cultures, combined with the ever-evolving development, that has prodded the growing interest for Southern cooking in urban areas across America.

Types of Southern Cuisine

The cooking procedures in the southern region of the U.S. are as diverse as the items used to prepare the food. These style of cooking get their foundations from the British, African, Irish, Native American, Spanish, and French impacts.

Some of the most notable sorts of Southern Cuisine are cajun, low country, creole, soul food, and Floribbean cooking. In ongoing history, components of the Southern cooking have spread north, affecting the evolvement of different varieties of American cooking.

Cajun cuisine originated from the relatives of French Canadians, otherwise known as Arcadians who relocated to Southern Louisiana during the 1700s. Boudin sausage, chicken giblets rice, and jambalaya are mainstream Cajun dishes.

Creole cuisine is a style of food preparation related to cooking procedures from Spain and France, utilizing seasoning and spices from Africa, and, Native American Indians.

Floribbean cuisine is uniquely different from the remaining types of Southern cuisine. Floribbean cooking is a combination of Spanish, Haitian, and Cuban styles of cooking.

Gullah cuisine originated from ex-slaves who moved after the Civil War to the Beach front regions and Sea Islands of Georgia, South Carolina, and Northeast Florida. Numerous culinary history specialists believe that the Gullah style of cooking is practically indistinguishable from West African food.

Low Country cuisine is based majorly on the utilization of rice, and the region incorporates the coastal fields of South Carolina. For more than 200 years, rice was classified as "Carolina Gold" here, because it made numerous ranch proprietors rich during the Antebellum Period.

Soul Food is a genuinely new name used to depict a specific style of Southern cooking. The term was derived during the 1960s, during The Civil Rights Movement, when African-Americans began to embrace their African social legacy, including Southern cooking.

Advantages of the Southern Cuisine

Several medical advantages can be gotten from the nourishing ingredients utilized in these southern cooking customary kinds of cooking.

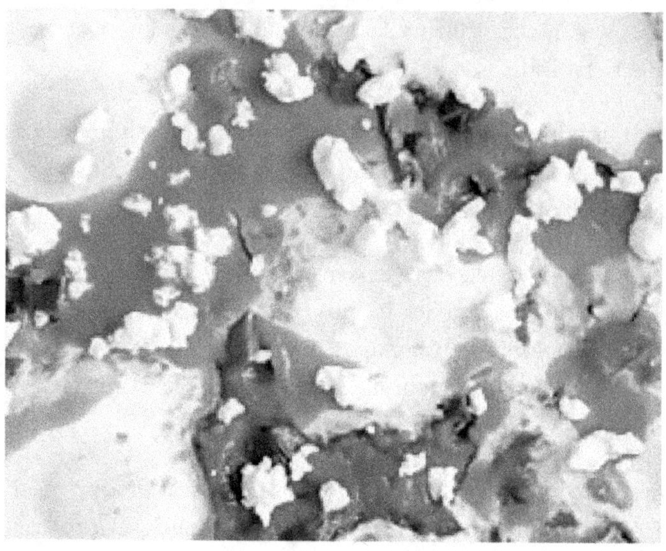

- Amazing wellspring of nutrients and minerals

- Excellent source of manganese, calcium, iron, and omega 3 fatty acids

- Contain various phytonutrients, which plays a part in preventing ovarian and breast cancer

- Delicious wellsprings of beta carotene and various other minerals

- Balance out blood sugar levels and lower insulin opposition.

The Ketogenic Primer

The Ketogenic diet, or Keto diet, is a food methodology in which you radically reduce your carbohydrate intake and supplant it with fat to get your digestion to a state called ketosis.

The ketogenic diet is a low carbohydrate, high fat, moderate protein diet, that allows the body system to produces ketones in the liver rather than glucose which is the fundamental source of energy in the body which is referred to as a state of ketosis.

In ketosis, your body changes fat to fuel that is consumed for energy. At the point when you're in ketosis, your body is consuming fat for fuel. For the end goal for ketosis to occur, the body's production of glucose needs to be significantly cut short, at the point when your body runs out of glucose, at that point is when you enter ketosis.

Ketogenic targets low carb (under 5% of your aggregate), and focuses on a high-fat substance (70% of your eating routine). It wipes out grains, tubers, and most organic products due to the carbohydrate content.

Ketones and Ketosis

At the point when your body doesn't have carbohydrates/glucose to burn for energy, it will have to dive into your fat storage facility to get fuel. Without glucose, your liver takes your stored fat and separates it into usable components called ketone bodies, or ketones. These ketones can be utilized by your body for fuel.

There are three types of ketones, which are important for you to know about.

- Acetoacetate

- Beta-hydroxybutyrate

- Acetone

Advantages of the Ketogenic Diet

- Helps with weight reduction

- Used in the treatment of epilepsy

- Help with Type II diabetes, polycystic ovary disorder, skin inflammation

- Used to manage neurological sicknesses and some sorts of cancer

- Decreases the risk of respiratory and cardiovascular diseases

Creamy Velvet Pork Chops

Preparation Time: 8 minutes

Cook Time: 23 minutes

Servings: 4

Ingredients

1/2 cup cream

1 cup chicken broth

3 tablespoons butter

4 skinless & boneless pork chops

salt & pepper, to taste

Instructions

1. Using a large skillet, melt the butter over medium high heat then add in the pork chops seasoned with salt & pepper.

2. Cook the pork until browned all over, flip halfway through cook time.

3. Pour the chicken broth into the skillet then reduce the heat and cook for 10 minutes until the broth is reduced by half.

4. Turn off the heat and remove the pork from the skillet then pour in the cream and stir cook over low heat until warm and thick.

5. Serve the pork chops drizzled with the cream sauce and enjoy.

Nutrition Information

Calories: 627kcal | Fat: 27.6g | Carbohydrates: 23.6g | Protein: 89.6g

Pulled Crock Pot Pork

Preparation Time: 5 minutes

Cook Time: 8 hours

Servings: 8

Ingredients

1/2 teaspoon cumin

1 juiced orange

1 teaspoon oregano

1 diced yellow onion

2 tablespoons paprika

4 minced garlic cloves

4 1/2 pounds' pork shoulder

salt & pepper, to taste

Instructions

1. Using a large crock pot, pour in the juiced orange, garlic, onion and set aside.

2. With a small mixing bowl, add in all the spices and mix together.

3. Cut excess fat from the pork then coat with the spice mixture and place inside the crock pot.

4. Cook the pork on low setting got 8 hours then transfer the pork until a cutting board and shred.

5. Serve and enjoy as desired.

Nutrition Information

Calories: 251kcal | Fat: 11g | Carbohydrates: 4g | Protein: 31g

Sirloin Steak Kabobs

Preparation Time: 12 minutes

Cook Time: 30 minutes

Servings: 2

Ingredients

1 bottle of marinade

1-pound cherry tomatoes, chopped into 1"

2 pounds' top sirloin

2 large onions, chopped into wedges

a handful of small mushrooms

Instructions

1. Use kitchen shears to dice the beef into bite size cubes then transfer into a large Ziploc bag.

2. Pour the marinade mixture into the bag, seal and refrigerate for an hour until marinated.

3. Heat the oven up to 350°F then soak 12 wooden skewers in water.

4. Thread the soaked skewers with the tomatoes, beef, mushrooms and onions until all the ingredients are finished.

5. Arrange the sewn kabobs on a baking sheet then bake in the oven for 30 minutes until the beef is lightly browned, flipping every 10 minutes.

6. Serve and enjoy as desired.

Nutrition Information

Calories: 185kcal | Fat: 6.4g | Carbohydrates: 16g | Protein: 15.4g

Crock Pot Sirloin Steak Roast

Preparation Time: 30 minutes

Cook Time: 8 hours

Servings: 4

Ingredients

1-pound sirloin steak

1 teaspoon dried oregano

1 tablespoon ground turmeric

1 1/2 tablespoons apple cider vinegar

2 tablespoons vegetable oil

3 tablespoons unsalted butter

sea salt, to taste

Instructions

1. Combine the turmeric, salt & oregano together then use to generously coat the steak.

2. Place the coated steak into a crock pot then pour on the vegetable oil.

3. Add in the butter and cook until the steak is tenderized for 6-8 hours over low heat.

4. Once cooked, shred the steak then coat with the cider vinegar.

Nutrition Information

Calories: 515kcal | Fat: 42.1g | Carbohydrates: 1.5g | Protein: 32.2g

Soy Sauced Fresh Ham

Preparation Time: 10 minutes

Cook Time: 10 minutes

Servings: 10

Ingredients

15 pounds whole fresh ham

soy sauce

house seasoning

Instructions

1. Heat the oven up to 325°F.

2. Generously coat the ham with the soy sauce and house seasoning.

3. Transfer the ham into the oven and bake until cooked through for 20 minutes per pound.

4. Allow the cooked ham to rest before slicing.

5. Serve and enjoy.

Nutrition Information

Calories: 808kcal | Fat: 28g | Carbohydrates: 16.3g | Protein: 113g

Slow Cooked Chuck Roast

Preparation Time: 5 minutes

Cook Time: 8 hours

Servings: 8

Ingredients

1 stick salted butter

1-ounce pack Au Jus gravy

1-ounce pack ranch dressing mix

4-pound beef chuck roast

a jar of drained pepperoncini peppers

Instructions

1. Place the chuck roast into a slow cooker then season with the dressing mix and gravy.

2. Pour in the pepperoncini & butter stick then cook for 6-8 hours on low heat.

3. Check for desired doneness then shred, serve and enjoy as desired.

Nutrition Information

Calories: 332kcal | Fat 21.8g | Carbohydrate 0.6g | Protein 34.3g

Simple Ketchup Meat Loaf

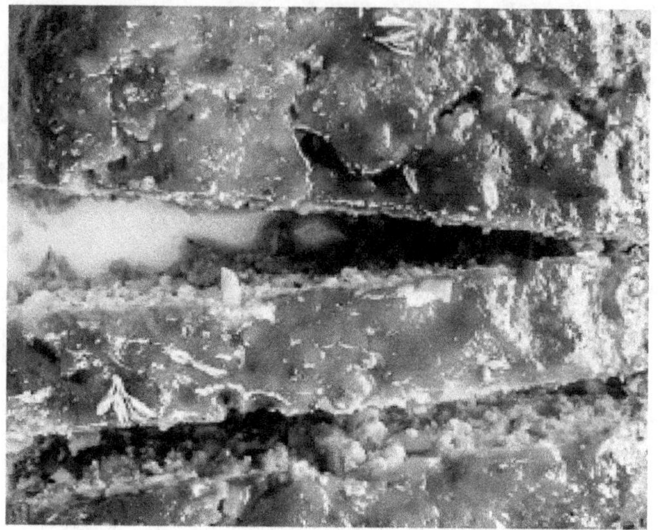

Preparation Time: 5 minutes

Cook Time: 45 minutes

Servings: 4

Ingredients

1/3 cup ketchup

1/3 cup diced red onions

1/3 teaspoon ground pepper

1/2 cup crumbled pork rinds

1 tablespoon Worcestershire sauce

1 1/2 pounds ground beef

1 1/2 teaspoons chili powder

1 1/2 teaspoons ground mustard

2 large eggs

2 teaspoons minced garlic cloves

4 ounces tomato sauce

Instructions

1. Heat the oven up to 375°F.

2. Add all the ingredients (except the ketchup) into a large mixing bowl and combine together.

3. Transfer the mixture into a large loaf pan then press down and mold into shape.

4. Place the pan into the oven and bake for 45 minutes until done as desired.

5. Coat the top of the loaf with the ketchup, cut, serve and enjoy.

Nutrition Information

Calories: 472kcal | Fat 25g | Carbohydrates 5.08g | Protein 52.75g

Simple Keto Meatloaf

Preparation Time: 5 minutes

Cook Time: 1 hour

Servings: 8

Ingredients

1/2 teaspoon powdered garlic

1/2 cup ketchup, no sugar added

1 tablespoon powdered onion

1 teaspoon dry ground mustard

1 1/2 tablespoons Worcestershire sauce

2 pounds ground beef

3 large eggs

salt & pepper, to taste

Instructions

1. Heat the oven up to 350°F then add all the ingredients (except the ketchup) into a mixing bowl and combine together.

2. Mold the batter into a loaf shape then place inside a baking dish and bake for 45 minutes.

3. Take the meatloaf out of the oven and scoop some of the dripping over it then top with the ketchup until evenly covered.

4. Return the loaf into the oven and bake for an extra 15 minutes.

5. Allow the loaf to cool off then slice, serve and enjoy.

Nutrition Information

Calories: 283kcal | Fat: 19g | Carbohydrates: 2g | Protein: 24g

Sausage Gravy Steak Cube

Preparation Time: 30 minutes

Cook Time: 25 minutes

Servings: 4

Ingredients

for the cubed steak

1/4 cup heavy cream

1/2 cup shredded parmesan cheese

1 teaspoon paprika

1 pound cubed steak

1 1/2 cups crushed pork rinds

1 1/2 teaspoon powdered onion

1 1/2 teaspoon powdered garlic

2 large eggs

a pinch of cayenne pepper

sea salt & black pepper, to taste

vegetable oil

for the gravy

1/2 cups heavy cream

1/2 teaspoon sea salt

2/3 cup diced onion

1 tablespoon chopped parsley

2 tablespoons butter

3 minced garlic cloves

12 ounces' pork sausage

Instructions

1. Generously season the cubed steak with salt and pepper then set aside.

2. With a large mixing bowl, add in the eggs, heavy cream and combine together.

3. Pour the parmesan cheese, pork rinds, powdered garlic & onion, cayenne pepper & paprika into a mixing bowl and combine then pour into a large plate to a thin layer.

4. Using a large skillet, pour in 1/2" of oil and heat over medium high heat.

5. Dredge the cubed steak in the egg & cream mixture then run through the cheese mix until coated and fry in the hot oil for 3 minutes per side until crispy & golden brown.

6. Once done add the gravy butter into the skillet and melt then add in the sausage and cook until browned.

7. Remove the sausage from the skillet and set aside then add the garlic & onion into the remaining dripping in the skillet and cook until tenderized over low heat.

8. Pour the heavy cream into the skillet, add in the parsley, season with the salt and boil over medium heat then reduce and simmer until thickened.

9. Add the sausage back into the pan and combine.

Serve the browned steak cubes with a coating of the gravy and enjoy.

Nutrition Information

Calories: 676kcal | Fat: 51g | Carbohydrate: 5g | Protein: 47g

Fried Bacon Cabbage

Preparation Time: 20 minutes

Cook Time 45 minutes

Servings: 8

Ingredients

1/2 teaspoon paprika

1 sliced large sweet onion

1 shredded large cabbage head

4 minced garlic cloves

8 bacon slices

wholesome yum sweeteners

sea salt & black pepper, to taste

Instructions

1. Using a large sauté pan, add the bacon into the pan in a single layer.

2. Place the pan over a medium heat and heat until browned for 10 minutes, flipping after the first 5 minutes.

3. Take the bacon out of the pan then add the onion into the remaining bacon grease in the pan and sauté for 10 minutes until browned.

4. Create some space in the center of the pan then add in the minced garlic and sauté until fragrant for a minute then mix with the browned onions.

5. Add the chopped cabbage into the pan, mix with the onions and cabbage then season with salt, pepper paprika and toss together.

6. Cover the pan and cook until the cabbage is tenderized for 15-25 minutes.

7. Meanwhile, chop the bacon into bits then return back into the pan once the cabbage is tenderized and stir together.

8. Serve and enjoy as desired.

Nutrition Information

Calories: 143kcal | Fat: 9g | Carbohydrates: 12g | Protein: 5g

POULTRY RECIPES

Air Fried Keto Chicken

Preparation Time: 20 minutes

Cook Time: 15 minutes

Servings: 6

Ingredients

1/2 cup almond meal

1/2 teaspoon powdered hot chili

1/2 cup shredded parmesan cheese

1 large egg

1 teaspoon dried oregano

1 teaspoon powdered garlic

2 teaspoons celery salt

2 tablespoons heavy cream

2 pounds' chicken thigh fillets

Instructions

1. Chop the chicken thighs into 3 even sizes then place in a large mixing bowl.

2. Combine the oregano, powdered chili & garlic and salt together then pour over the chopped chicken fillet and toss until well coated.

3. Set the coated chicken fillets aside to marinate for 30 minutes.

4. In the meantime, combine the heavy cream and egg together then add the parmesan cheese and almond flour into a separate bowl and mix together.

5. Transfer the cheese mixture into a baking tray then heat a deep fryer up to 180°C.

6. Once marinated, dredge each of the chicken piece in the cream mixture then run through the almond meal mix.

7. Arrange the breaded chicken pieces on a tray then place on a fryer basket and air fry until golden brown for 5-7 minutes.

8. Check for desired doneness then serve and enjoy.

Nutrition Information

Calories: 359kcal | Fat: 18g | Carbohydrates: 1g | Protein: 44g

Cheese Lime Chicken Breasts

Preparation Time: 25 minutes

Cook Time: 35 minutes

Servings: 4

Ingredients

1/4 teaspoon dried basil

1/2 cup butter

1/2 cup shredded parmesan cheese

1 juiced lime

3 tablespoons mayonnaise

4 skinless & boneless chicken breasts

salt, to taste

lime, to garnish

Instructions

1. Place the chicken breast in a Ziploc bag then pour in the lime juice and refrigerate for an hour to marinate.

2. Pour 1/4 cup of the butter into a large skillet and melt over medium high heat.

3. Add in the marinated chicken breast and cook for 20 minutes until browned.

4. With a small mixing bowl, add in the remaining butter, basil, salt, parmesan cheese, mayonnaise and mix until combined.

5. Transfer the cooked chicken onto a baking sheet then generously cover with the cheese mixture.

6. Bake the cheese coated chicken in the oven at 350°F for 10 minutes until the cheese melts.

7. Serve and enjoy with a garnish of the lime.

Nutrition Information

Calories: 1016kcal | Fat: 48.6g | Carbohydrates: 1.9g | Protein: 142.3g

Marinated Brown Chicken Breast

Preparation Time: 20 minutes

Cook Time: 20 minutes

Servings: 3

Ingredients

6 boneless & skinless chicken breasts

vegetable oil, to fry

a bottle of salad dressing

Instructions

1. Add the chicken breast into a large Ziploc bag then cover with the salad dressing.

2. Place the Ziploc bag in the refrigerator and allow to marinate for 1 hour.

3. Pour the oil into a large skillet and heat over medium high heat until hot.

4. Place the marinated chicken into the hot oil and cook for 10 minutes until browned.

5. Flip the chicken over and brown the other side for another 10 minutes.

6. Check the chicken for desired doneness then serve and enjoy.

Calories: 801kcal | Fat: 27g | Carbohydrates: 1.2g | Protein: 138.5g

Fried Chicken Leg

Preparation Time: 12 minutes

Cook Time: 18 minutes

Servings: 6

Ingredients

1 teaspoon paprika

1 cup coconut flour

1 teaspoon powdered garlic

5 pounds' chicken leg quarters

salt & pepper, to taste

vegetable oil, for frying

Instructions

1. Using a large mixing bowl, add in the chicken leg, powdered garlic, pepper, salt, paprika and combine together.

2. Massage the spices into the chicken until fully coated then place in the refrigerator for 1 hour to marinate.

3. Generously coat the marinated chicken legs in the coconut flour then pour the oil into a deep fryer and heat up to 375°F.

4. Add the batches into the fryer in batches and cook until crispy and golden brown for 8 minutes per side.

5. Check for desired doneness then serve and enjoy.

Nutrition Information

Calories: 425kcal | Fat: 32g | Carbohydrates: 1g | Protein: 34g

Baked Smokehouse Chicken

Preparation Time: 15 minutes

Cook Time: 1 hour 15 minutes

Servings: 4

Ingredients

1 tablespoon hot sauce

1 teaspoon smoked paprika

1 teaspoon crushed red pepper flakes

1 cup cider vinegar, with extra 1/2 cup

3 tablespoons brown sugar

4 skinless & boneless chicken thighs

salt & black pepper, to taste

Instructions

1. Add all the ingredients (except the chicken) into a baking dish and combine together until the sugar is dissolved.

2. Place the chicken thighs into the dish, cover and bake in the oven for 45 minutes at 300°F.

3. Flip the chicken over and bake for another 45 minutes then uncover and broil for 20 minutes until crispy and browned.

4. Serve and enjoy with a drizzle of the dish juices.

Nutrition Information

Calories: 186kcal | Fat: 6.4g | Carbohydrates: 11.1g | Protein: 19.6g

Swiss Tender Potatoes Drumsticks

Preparation Time: 30 minutes

Cook Time: 1 hour 30 minutes

Servings: 6

Ingredients

1/3 cup juice lime

1/3 cup vegetable oil

1 tablespoon dried oregano

2 teaspoons powdered garlic

4 pounds' chicken drumsticks

10 small red potatoes

salt & black pepper, to taste

Instructions

1. Using a small mixing bowl, add in all the dry ingredients and combine together.

2. Rinse, dry and chop the potatoes into quarters.

3. Place the potatoes and drumsticks into a large baking dish then season with the seasonings mix.

4. Drizzle the seasoned chicken and potatoes with the lime juice and vegetable oil then over the pan with foil.

5. Place the pan in the oven and bake for 1 hour at 350°F.

6. Remove the foil then bake again for 30 minutes until slightly browned at 400°F.

7. Serve and enjoy.

Nutrition Information

Calories: 1088kcal | Fat: 50.7g | Carbohydrates: 75.6g | Protein: 75.3g

Roasted Turkey with Gravy Dip

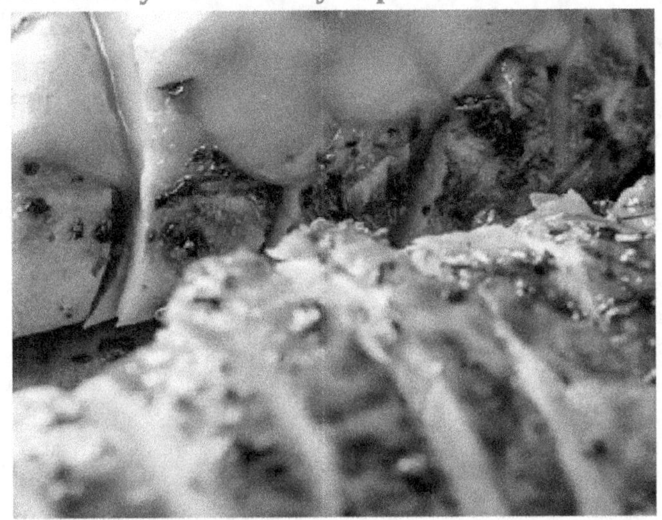

Preparation Time: 20 minutes

Cook Time: 3 hours 15 minutes

Servings: 18

Ingredients

1/4 cup cornstarch

1/3 cup water

1/2 cup melted butter

1 diced onion

1 minced garlic clove

2 bay leaves

2 teaspoons chopped fresh herbs

14 pounds' turkey

14 ounces can chicken broth

kosher salt & black pepper, to taste

Instructions

1. heat the oven up to 325°F then massage the salt & pepper into the turkey cavity.

2. Place the garlic, onion, bay leaves & chopped herbs into the turkey cavity then coat with half of the butter.

3. Season the turkey with extra salt & pepper then truss if desired.

4. Place the turkey on an aluminum foil then roast for 2 hours 30 minutes.

5. Remove the foil and coat with the remaining butter then roast for another 45 minutes at 425°F, covering during the last 15 minutes.

6. In the meantime, discard the fat from the pan juices then pour in the broth, remaining pepper, and thyme into the remaining juices in the pan.

7. Place the pan over medium heat and simmer for 3 minutes.

8. Combine the water and cornstarch together then strain the gravy into a small pot and place over low heat.

9. Gently whisk the cornstarch mixture into strained gravy and simmer until thickened for 2 minutes.

10. Serve and enjoy the turkey with the gravy mix.

Nutrition Information

Calories: 170kcal | Fat: 5.5g | Carbohydrates: 2.1g | Protein: 23.4g

Air Fried Chicken Tenders

Preparation Time: 8 minutes

Cook Time: 10 minutes

Servings: 4

Ingredients

1/2 cup almond flour

1 beaten large egg

1 teaspoon paprika

1-pound chicken tenders

1 teaspoon powdered garlic

salt & pepper, to taste

Instructions

1. Generously coat a fryer basket with cooking oil spray.

2. Sprinkle the chicken tenders with the salt & pepper then dredge in the almond flour, whisked egg and flour again.

3. Place the chicken into the fryer basket then air fry at 350°F for 5 minutes.

4. Flip the chicken over and cook for an extra 5 minutes.

5. Check for desired doneness, serve and enjoy.

Nutrition Information

Calories: 58kcal | Fat: 1.9g | Carbohydrates: 1.8g | Protein: 6.2g

Crockpot Cream Cheese Chicken

Preparation Time: 10 minutes

Cook Time: 5 hours

Servings: 10

Ingredients

1 teaspoon dried dill

1 tablespoon dried parsley

1 bunch diced green onions

1 teaspoon crushed red pepper

1 1/2 cups cheddar

1 1/2 teaspoons powdered onion

2 pounds' chicken breast

2 tablespoons dried chives

2 teaspoons powdered garlic

2 (8 ounces) pack cream cheese

8 bacon slices

salt & pepper, to taste

Instructions

1. Fry the bacon until crispy then place the chicken breast into the crockpot and season with the spices.

2. Cover the chicken breast with the cream cheese then cover the pot and cook for 5 hours on high settings and 7 hours on low settings.

3. Once cooked, shred the chicken then add in the diced onions, fried bacon, cheddar cheese, then combine together then serve and enjoy.

Nutrition Information

Calories: 394kcal | Fat 29.1g | Carbohydrate 3.7g | Protein 28.4g

Ketogenic Chicken and Dumplings

Preparation Time: 10 minutes

Cook Time: 40 minutes

Servings: 2

Ingredients

for the dumplings

1/4 teaspoon wheat gluten

1/4 teaspoon herbes de provence

1-ounce cream cheese

2 large eggs

for the chicken

1 cup chicken stock

1 teaspoon vegetable oil

1 tablespoon diced onion

1 pound chopped chicken breast

2 tablespoons chopped celery

salt & pepper, to taste

for the sauce

1/4 cup heavy cream

1/4 cup chicken stock

1/4 teaspoon herbes de provence

1 tablespoon butter

1-ounce cream cheese

Instructions

for the dumpling

1. Heat the oven up to 325°F then add all the dumpling ingredients into a high speed blender and process until blended.

2. Prepare a baking dish with a large parchment paper then pour the batter into the dish and bake until firm and set for 20-25 minutes.

3. Remove the batter from dish and allow to cool off then cut into squares and set aside.

for the chicken

4. Pour the vegetable oil into a large sauté pan and heat up until hot then add in the chicken, celery, onions and sauté until the veggies are tenderized.

5. Pour the chicken stock into the sauté pan and simmer over medium high heat.

6. Pour in the chopped dumplings, cover and simmer for 10-15 minutes

7. Uncover the pan and allow the chicken stock to boil not dry off.

8. In the meantime, pour in the sauce chicken stock into a small microwave save bowl, add in the cream cheese, heavy cream and microwave for a minute then whisk until smooth.

9. Pour the cream mixture into the chicken pan, add in the herbes de Provence and butter then stir occasionally as it simmers until thickened and reduced for 10 minutes.

10. Taste and season with salt & pepper as desired then serve and enjoy with a garnish of parsley.

Nutrition Information

Calories: 647kcal | Fat: 40g | Carbohydrates: 3g | Protein: 60g

RICE, NOODLES & PASTA RECIPES

Shirataki Noodles & Shrimps Pad

Preparation Time: 8 minutes

Cook Time: 12 minutes

Servings: 3

Ingredients

1/4 teaspoon crushed red pepper

1/2 cup chopped cilantro

1 lemon juice & zest

1 minced garlic clove

1 teaspoon cashew butter

1 1/2 tablespoons divided vegetable oil

2 beaten large eggs

2 diced green onions

2 tablespoons coconut aminos

2 (7 ounce) pack shirataki fettuccini noodles

4 chopped cashews

18 medium shrimp

sea salt, to taste

Instructions

1. Prepare the noodles according to the packet instructions then drain and set aside.

2. Using a small mixing bowl, add in the 3/4 tablespoons of oil, cashew butter, 1/2 lemon juice, coconut aminos, minced garlic, crushed pepper, combine and set aside.

3. Place a large skillet over medium heat then pour in the remaining oil and cook the shrimp seasoned with salt for 2 minutes on each side.

4. Move the prepared shrimp to a side of the skillet then pour the beaten eggs into the other side and scramble for a minute.

5. Add the prepared noodles, aminos sauce mixture, diced onions & cilantro into the skillet then toss together until incorporated and heat through until warm.

6. Drizzle the entire mixture with the remaining lemon juice then taste and adjust for seasoning.

7. Serve and enjoy with a garnish of crushed cashews.

Nutrition Information

Calories: 180kcal | Fat: 12g | Carbohydrates: 5g | Protein: 12g

Pasta & Shrimp Piccata

Preparation Time: 10 minutes

Cook Time: 20 minutes

Servings: 4

Ingredients

1/4 teaspoon powdered garlic

1/2 lime zest

1/2 cup juiced lime

1/2 cup chicken stock

1 chopped lime

1 diced shallot

1 pound peeled & deveined shrimp

2 tablespoons butter

2 minced garlic cloves

3 tablespoons capers

4 tablespoons ghee

4 spiralized zucchinis

a handful of chopped parsley

salt & black pepper, to taste

Instructions

1. Squeeze the chopped zucchini to remove excess water then heat the butter over medium heat in a large saucepan.

2. Once melted, generously coat the shrimp with the garlic powder & salt then place into the hot & melted butter and cook until pink for 2 minutes on each side.

3. Take the shrimp out of the pan and set aside then add in the shallot & garlic and sauté until fragrant for 3 minutes.

4. Add in the ghee and melt then pour in the chicken stock, lime juice & zest and bring to a low boil, scraping any brown bits from the bottom of the pan.

5. Add in the chopped lime, capers and cook until the lime is tenderized for 5 minutes over low heat.

6. Add in the zoodles & shrimps then toss around until well coated and cook until the noodles are tenderized & shrimp heated through for 3 minutes.

7. Serve and enjoy with a season of the black pepper and garnish of parsley.

Nutrition Information

Calories: 412kcal | Fat: 22.1g | Carbohydrates: 9.9g | Protein: 26.3g

Bacon & Sage Carbonara Zoodles

Preparation Time: 20 minutes

Cook Time: 30 minutes

Servings: 3

Ingredients

1/4 cup chicken broth

1/2 teaspoon turmeric

1 cups chopped bacon

1 cup butternut squash

2 cups cauliflower

3 cups zucchini noodles

3 tablespoons melted butter

salt, to taste

a handful of chopped sage leaves

Instructions

1. Using a small saucepan, steam the cauliflower & butternut squash until cooked through and tenderized.

2. Fry the chopped bacon over medium heat until crispy and golden then transfer onto a serving plate to cool.

3. Add the sage leaves into the fry pan and cook with the bacon fat until crispy then transfer into the plates with bacon.

4. Transfer the steamed cauliflower into a high speed blender.

5. Add in the butter, turmeric, 2 tablespoons of broth, salt and process until smooth & creamy.

6. Add in extra broth until a desired consistency is achieved.

7. Divide the zucchini noodles into 2 serving plates then top with the creamy mixture, a garnish of the crispy bacon & sage leaves.

8. Season with salt as desired then serve and enjoy.

Nutrition Information

Calories: 397kcal | Fat: 29.5g | Carbohydrates: 17.5g | Protein: 18.5g

Broccoli & Cauliflower Chicken Casserole

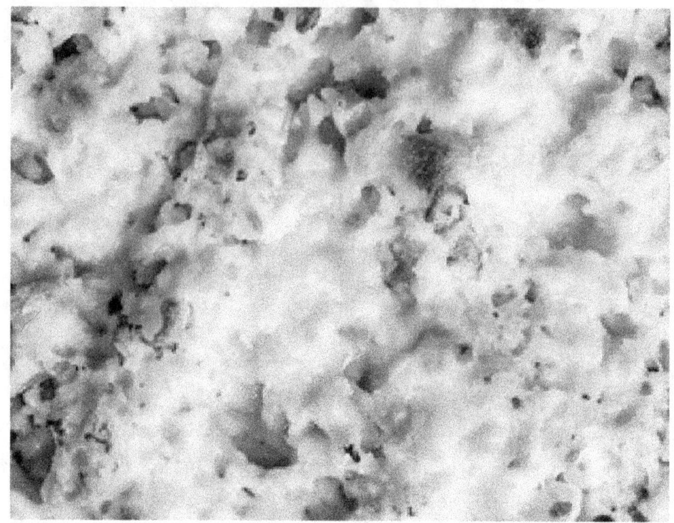

Preparation Time: 10 minutes

Cook Time: 30 minutes

Servings: 6

Ingredients

1/4 teaspoon powdered garlic & onion

2 cups cauliflower florets

2 tablespoons vegetable oil

2 tablespoons parmesan cheese

2 cups cooked & shredded chicken breasts

3 ounces' cheddar cheese

3 cups broccoli florets

salt & pepper, to taste

Instructions

1. Heat the oven up to 400°F then boil the cauliflower florets until tenderized then drain.

2. Microwave the broccoli florets until cooked then combine with the chopped chicken.

3. Pour the cooled cauliflower florets into a high speed blender then add in the spices, parmesan cheese, vegetable oil and blend until smooth & combined.

4. Add the cauliflower sauce into the broccoli and chicken mix then transfer into a baking dish.

5. Top the chicken mix with the cheddar cheese and bake in the oven for 20 minutes.

6. Serve and enjoy as desired.

Nutrition Information

Calories: 233kcal | Fat: 20.4g | Carbohydrates: 2.2g | Protein: 11.3g

Sausage & Shrimp Rice

Preparation Time: 30 minutes

Cook Time: 55 minutes

Servings: 4

Ingredients

1/4 cup fresh parsley

1/4 cup diced green onions

1/4 teaspoon cayenne, if desired

1/2 juiced lime

1 tablespoon ghee

1 cup chopped celery

1 diced medium onion

1-pound medium shrimp

1 teaspoon dried thyme

1 teaspoon dried oregano

1 tablespoon vegetable oil

1 chopped & cored red bell pepper

1 chopped & cored green bell pepper

2 bay leaves

2 cups chicken stock

2 minced garlic cloves

2 tablespoons tomato paste

3 cups cooked cauliflower rice

12 ounces chopped andouille sausage

14 ounces can tomatoes, chopped

kosher salt & black pepper, to taste

Instructions

1. Using a large sauté pot, pour in the oil and heat up to a medium heat until hot.

2. Add in the sausage and sauté until browned then remove, crumble and set aside.

3. Pour the ghee into the sauté pot then add in the peppers, celery, onion and sauté until translucent for 10 minutes.

4. Pour in the chopped tomatoes, thyme, oregano, cayenne pepper, garlic, tomato paste and cook until the veggies are combined together.

5. Pour the chicken stock into the pot then bring the mixture to a boil.

6. Add the crumbled sausage into the pot with the bay leaves, salt & pepper then boil again and simmer and low heat for 15 minutes.

7. Add 2 tablespoons of parsley green onion, juiced lime and shrimps into the pot then stir to mix.

8. Take the pot off from the heat and allow to steam until the shrimp is cooked for 15 minutes.

9. Serve the cauliflower rice topped with the shrimps' mixture, garnished with parsley, green onions and enjoy.

Nutrition Information

Calories: 981kcal | Fat: 56g | Carbohydrates: 51.9g | Protein: 63.6g

Cider Vinegar Pasta Dough

Preparation Time: 30 minutes

Cook Time: 5 minutes

Servings: 4

Ingredients

for the dough

1 lightly beaten egg

2 teaspoons water

2 teaspoons xanthan gum

2 teaspoons apple cider vinegar

24g coconut flour

96g almond flour

salt, to taste

to fry

4 minced garlic cloves

56g butter

Instructions

1. Using a high speed blender, add in the coconut & almond flour, salt & xanthan gum then process until combined.

2. Pour the cider vinegar into the blender, once blended, pour in the beaten egg, water in bits and process until the dough is mixed, firmed and a ball is formed.

3. Transfer the dough mixture into a cling film and knead then transfer into the refrigerator and allow to rest for 30 minutes.

4. Roll the mixture out into its thinnest point then cut out into a 2" by 1" rectangle and freeze for 15 extra minutes.

5. Pour the butter into a large skillet then heat up over low heat until hot then add in the minced garlic and cook until fragrant and translucent.

6. Add in the shaped dough and baste until tenderized and with some color then check for desired doneness and take off the heat.

7. Serve and enjoy with a topping of choice.

Nutrition Information

Calories 176kcal | Fat: 13g | Carbohydrates: 8g | Protein: 7g

Simple Shrimp Scampi

Preparation Time: 12 minutes

Cook Time: 18 minutes

Servings: 2

Ingredients

1 lime zest, chopped into wedges

2 tablespoons ghee

2 minced garlic cloves

2 tablespoons vegetable oil

2 spiralized medium zucchini

6 deveined jumbo shrimp

salt, to taste

a handful of chopped parsley

diced green onion, to garnish

Instructions

1. Using a large skillet, pour in the ghee and heat over medium heat.

2. Add the shrimp into the hot ghee and cook for 2 minutes until the color starts to change then flip and cook the other side.

3. Repeat the same process with the remaining shrimp if cooking in batches then set aside.

4. Add the minced garlic into the skillet and cook until tenderized for 2 minutes.

5. Add in the spiralized zucchini and tenderize for 2 minutes then return the shrimp back into the pan and take off the heat.

6. Pour in the vegetable oil, lime zest and zest together.

7. Divide the shrimp scampi between 2 serving plates then top with the diced onions & parsley and a drizzle of lime.

8. Season with salt & pepper to taste then serve and enjoy.

Nutrition Information

Calories: 335kcal | Fat: 26.1g | Carbohydrates: 6.1g | Protein: 19g

Beef, Broccoli and Rice

Preparation Time: 15 minutes

Cook Time: 25 minutes

Servings: 4

Ingredients

1/4 cup soy sauce

1/4 teaspoon black pepper

1-pound sirloin, chopped into thin strips

2 teaspoons minced garlic

2 tablespoons cornstarch

3 tablespoons vegetable oil

4 cups broccoli florets

cooked brown rice

Instructions

1. Pour 2 tablespoons of oil into a large skillet and heat over medium high heat.

2. Combine the black pepper and cornstarch together then coat the beef strips in the mixture.

3. Place the coated strips into the skillet and cook for 5 minutes until the meat is browned, occasionally stirring.

4. Remove the beef from the skillet, set aside and reduce the heat to medium.

5. Pour the remaining oil into the skillet then add in the garlic, broccoli florets and cook for 4 minutes until the broccoli is tenderized.

6. Add the beef back into the skillet, pour in the soy sauce, 1/3 cup of water and cook for 4 minutes until thickened, occasionally stirring.

7. Serve and enjoy with the prepared brown rice.

Nutrition Information

Calories: 546kcal | Fat: 20g | Carbohydrates: 38.2g | Protein: 54.4g

Cream & Broth Smashed Cauliflower

Preparation Time: 5 minutes

Cook Time: 5 minutes

Servings: 5

Ingredients

1/3 cup chicken broth

1 medium cauliflower head

2 tablespoons sour cream

salt & pepper, to taste

a handful of chopped chives

Instructions

1. Chop the cauliflower into florets then simmer until tenderized.

2. Add the prepared cauliflower into a high speed blender then pour in the sour cream, salt & pepper, and chicken broth.

3. Pulse the blender until the mixture is combined and smooth.

4. Serve the smashed florets mix with a garnish of the chives and enjoy.

Nutrition Information

Calories: 61kcal | Fat: 1.6g | Carbohydrates: 8.1g | Protein: 4g

Chicken & Rice Noodles Lettuce Wraps

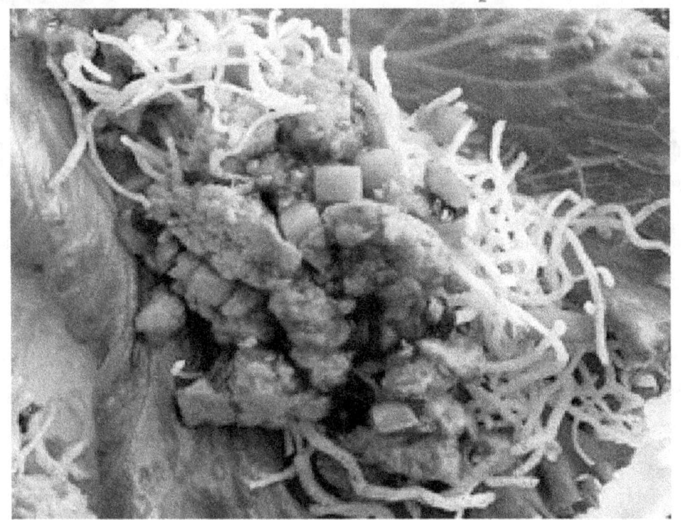

Preparation Time: 18 minutes

Cook Time: 25 minutes

Servings: 3

Ingredients

1 cup chopped mushrooms

2 tablespoons brown sugar

3 diced green onions

3 tablespoons soy sauce

3 skinless & boneless chicken breasts, chopped into bites

rice sticks

vegetable oil, to cook

a bunch of lettuce head

a small can of chopped water chestnuts

Instructions

1. Using a large skillet, pour in a tablespoon oil and heat up over medium heat.

2. Add the chicken pieces into the skillet and cook, occasionally stirring until cooked through.

3. Once done, remove the chicken from the heat and dice then combine the brown sugar and soy sauce in a mixing bowl.

4. Return the chicken back to the heat along with the water chestnuts, mushrooms, green onions then pour in the sauce mixture and stir cook until heated through over medium heat.

5. Using a small sauté pan, pour in some oil and heat up over medium heat then break the rice sticks into the pot.

6. Once puffed up, immediately transfer the sticks onto a paper towel to drain.

7. Serve the chicken bite mixture in with the lettuce leaves, top with the crunchy rice noodles and enjoy.

Nutrition Information

Calories: 950kcal | Fat: 19.6g | Carbohydrates: 53.4g | Protein: 140.7g

Bacon & Shrimp Cauliflower Grits

Preparation Time: 15 minutes

Cook Time: 30 minutes

Servings: 5

Ingredients

for the shrimp

1/2 chopped bell pepper

1/2 tablespoon minced garlic

1 tablespoon butter

1 tablespoon creole seasoning

1-pound large shrimp, peeled & deveined

2 teaspoons paprika

4 bacon slices

salt, to taste

for the sauce

1/4 cup heavy cream

1/2 cup low salt vegetable broth

1 teaspoon Worcestershire sauce

2 tablespoons cream cheese

2 teaspoon tabasco sauce, if desired

for the grits

1/4 cup heavy cream

1/2 cup unsweetened almond milk

1 cup shredded sharp cheddar cheese

2 tablespoons tomato paste

2 tablespoons butter

2 diced green onions, if desired

2 tablespoons crumbled goat cheese, if desired

4 cups cauliflower rice

Instructions

1. Using a small mixing bowl, add in the paprika, salt, creole seasoning and combine then add in the shrimp and toss around until coated then set aside.

2. Using a large skillet, add in the bacon slices and cook until crisp over medium high heat then take out of the skillet, crumble and keep aside.

3. Add a tablespoon of butter into the remaining bacon drippings in the skillet and sauté the garlic for 30 seconds then add in the chopped peppers and cook for 1 minute or two until tenderized.

4. Add in the shrimp and cook for 5 minutes until done then transfer the shrimp and peppers out of the pan and keep to the side.

5. Add all the sauce ingredients into the skillet content, whisk until combined and simmer until reduced by 1/4.

6. With a clean saucepan, pour in the heavy cream, almond milk, grits butter, tomato paste and heat over low heat until slightly boiled.

7. Take the pan of the heat then add in the cheeses and stir in until melted then pour in the cauliflower rice and stir to combine.

8. Return the mixture to the heat and simmer over low heat until done as desired.

9. Serve the cauliflower with a garnished of the shrimp & green onions drizzled with the sauce and topped with the crumbled cheese and bacon.

Nutrition Information

Calories: 415kcal | Fat: 26g | Carbohydrates: 8g | Protein: 31g

Simple Chicken Teriyaki Brown Rice

Preparation Time: 10 minutes

Cook Time: 20 minutes

Servings: 2

Ingredients

1/3 cup teriyaki sauce

1/2 teaspoon powdered garlic

1 tablespoon vegetable oil

1 pound skinless & boneless chicken breasts, chopped into bite size

2 cups broccoli

2 cups chopped carrots

2 cups cooked brown rice

Instructions

1. Pour the oil into a large skillet then place over medium high heat and heat until hot.

2. Add the chicken bites into the hot oil and cook for 5-7 minutes until slightly browned.

3. Pour in the teriyaki sauce, broccoli, carrots, powdered garlic and cook over medium heat for 10 minutes until the veggies are tenderized.

4. Serve and enjoy over the prepared brown rice.

Nutrition Information

Calories: 616kcal | Fat: 14.6g | Carbohydrates: 65.2g | Protein: 55.6g

Milk & Cheese Sauced Broccoli

Preparation Time: 15 minutes

Cook Time: 20 minutes

Servings: 2

Ingredients

1/4 stick butter

1 cup milk

1 tablespoon cornstarch

1 cup shredded cheddar cheese

2 large broccoli head

salt & pepper, to taste

Instructions

1. Using a small sauce pan, pour in the corn starch, milk and stir together then cook over medium heat until boil, stirring occasionally.

2. Reduce the heat to a low then add in the butter and stir until melted.

3. Pour in the cheese, pepper, salt and stir cook until the cheese melts and the sauce combined and smooth then set aside.

4. Prepare the broccoli in boiling water for 5 minutes until crisp tender then drain and serve.

5. Pour the milk cheese mixture over the prepared broccoli and enjoy.

Nutrition Information

Calories: 620kcal | Fat: 17.9g | Carbohydrates: 90.2g | Protein: 43.8g

Lime & Almond Garnished Broccolini

Preparation Time: 5 minutes

Cook Time: 10 minutes

Servings: 2

Ingredients

1/8 teaspoon red pepper flakes

1/4 teaspoon kosher salt

1/3 cup slivered almonds, toasted

1/2 teaspoon lime zest & juice

1 cooked bunch of broccolini

1 tablespoon vegetable oil

1 teaspoon minced garlic cloves

Instructions

1. Using a small skillet, pour in the vegetable oil and heat up over medium high heat.

2. Once hot, add in the garlic, pepper flakes and stir cook for 3 minutes until tenderized.

3. Serve the prepared broccolini and top with the pepper & garlic mixture.

4. Garnish the broccolini with salt, toasted almonds, lime juice & zest then toss together until coated.

5. Serve and enjoy as desired.

Nutrition Information

Calories: 221kcal | Fat: 17.7g | Carbohydrates: 11.2g | Protein: 4.1g

MAIN DISH & SOUP RECIPES

Tomato & Green Beans Soup

Preparation Time: 5 minutes

Cook Time: 20 minutes

Servings: 2

Ingredients

1 diced onion

2 (14.5 ounce) cans drained green beans

14.5 ounce can undrain diced tomatoes

salt & black pepper, to taste

Instructions

1. Using a small sauce pot, pour in the green beans then add in the tomatoes, diced onions, salt, pepper and stir to mix.

2. Bring the mixture to a light boil over medium high heat then reduce to a low heat and allow to simmer for 10 minutes.

3. Serve and enjoy.

Nutrition Information

Calories: 181kcal | Fat: 1.9g | Carbohydrates: 36.4g | Protein: 11.1g

Collard Greens Stew

Preparation Time: 5 minutes

Cook Time: 5 minutes

Servings: 5

Ingredients

1 butter stick

1 diced medium Vidalia onion

2 cups water

2 pounds chopped collard leaves

8 chopped bacon strips

salt & hot sauce, to taste

Instructions

1. Using a large saucepan, prepare the bacon slices over medium high heat for 5 minutes until crisp.

2. Add in the butter stick & onion and cook for 5 minutes until tenderized.

3. Pour in the water and simmer for 10 minutes then add in the collard leaves and cook for 20 minutes until tendered.

4. Season with salt & sauce as desired, toss together to combine then serve and enjoy.

Nutrition Information

Calories: 155kcal | Fat: 10g | Carbohydrates: 12.5g | Protein: 5.4g

Simple Chicken Noodles Soup

Preparation Time: 10 minutes

Cook Time: 15 minutes

Servings: 4

Ingredients

1/2 teaspoon dried basil

1/2 teaspoon dried oregano

3/4 cup diced green onion, only the green part

1 cup diced carrots

1 cup chopped celery

1 pound skinless & boneless chicken breast

2 tablespoons olive oil

2 cups spiralized noodles

6 cups chicken stock

salt & pepper, to taste

Instructions

1. Using an instant pot, pour in the olive oil and chicken breast into the pot bowl.

2. Sauté and cook until the chicken is cooked through for 10 minutes then shred with a fork.

3. Add in the diced onions, carrots & celery then cook for another 2 minutes.

4. Pour in the remaining ingredients, cover and push the soup setting set for 15 minutes.

5. Serve and enjoy with the prepared noodles.

Nutrition Information

Calories: 327kcal | Fat: 11g | Carbohydrates: 14.4g | Protein: 40g

Chicken & Cauliflower Soup

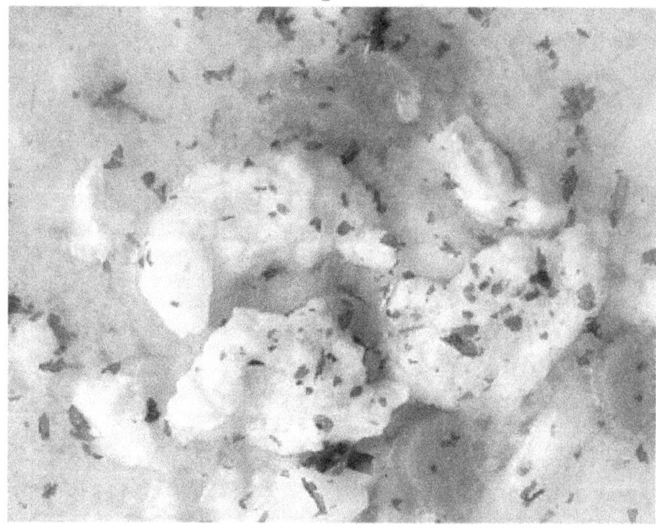

Preparation Time: 5 minutes

Cook Time: 30 minutes

Servings: 6

Ingredients

1/4 cup chopped parsley

1 bay leaf

1 diced small onion

1 teaspoon fresh thyme

1 boneless & skinless chicken breast

2 diced carrots

2 tablespoons butter

2 chopped celery stalks

2 cups riced cauliflower

2 cups canned coconut milk

4 cups chicken broth

salt and pepper, to taste

Instructions

1. Using a large soup pot, melt the butter over medium heat.

2. Add the diced carrot, onion & celery into the pot then cook until the veggies are tenderized for 5-8 minutes.

3. Season with salt & pepper then add in the thyme and stir.

4. Pour in the chicken stock with the bay leaf then bring to a boil and a low simmer.

5. Add in the chicken breast and simmer covered until the chicken is cooked through for 15 minutes.

6. Take the chicken breast out of the pot then shred with a fork and dispose of the bay leaf.

7. Return the chicken into the pot, pour in the riced cauliflower and simmer until the cauliflower is tenderized for 5 minutes.

8. Pour in the coconut milk, parsley and cook until heated through.

9. Season with salt & pepper then serve and enjoy.

Nutrition Information

Calories: 357kcal | Fat: 7.3g | Carbohydrates: 55.1g | Protein: 10.2g

Simple Taco Slow Cooked Soup

Preparation Time: 10 minutes

Cook Time: 4 hours

Servings: 8

Ingredients

1/4 teaspoon salt

1/2 cup diced onion

1/2 tablespoon juiced lime

1 teaspoon paprika

1 teaspoon chili powder

1 1/2 tablespoons cumin

2 pounds' chicken breasts

2 (10 ounce) cans tomatoes

2 (8 ounce) packs cream cheese

3 tablespoons juiced lemon

4 cups chicken broth

4 minced garlic cloves

to top

1 cup cheddar cheese

chopped jalapenos

a cup of sour cream

Instructions

1. Add the chicken breast into a slow cooker then garnish with the chopped onions, cumin, garlic, paprika, chili powder, lime & lemon juice, cans of tomatoes then pour in the chicken broth.

2. Cook on high setting for 4 hours then shred, pour in the cream cheese, stir and allow to heat through.

3. Serve and enjoy with a garnish of the topping ingredients.

Nutrition Information

Calories: 360kcal | Fat 23.1g | Carbohydrate 7.5g | Protein 30.6g

Bacon & Mayo Deviled Eggs

Preparation Time: 20 minutes

Cook Time: 10 minutes

Servings: 12

Ingredients

1/4 cup mayonnaise

1 tablespoon dried parsley flakes

2 diced & seeded cherry tomatoes

3 cooked & crumbled bacon slices

6 large hard-boiled eggs

salt & black pepper, to taste

Instructions

1. Vertically half the eggs and remove the yolks into a mixing bowl.

2. Add the parsley, tomatoes, bacon and mayonnaise into the bowl with the yolks and smash together.

3. Season the mixture with salt & pepper to taste then scoop into the halved eggs and garnish with extra bacon.

4. Serve and enjoy as desired or refrigerate for later.

Nutrition Information

Calories: 81kcal | Fat: 7g | Carbohydrates: 0.5g | Protein: 3.9g

Hot Savannah Crabmeat Dip

Preparation Time: 20 minutes

Cook Time: 40 minutes

Servings: 4

Ingredients

1/4 cup diced green onions

1/4 cup shredded Parmesan cheese

1/2 teaspoon dry mustard

3/4 cup mayonnaise

1-pound crabmeat

1 teaspoon hot sauce

1 cup shredded pepper jack cheese

2 tablespoons juiced lime

3 tablespoons Worcestershire sauce

6 minced garlic cloves

salt & pepper, to taste

Instructions

1. Heat the oven up to 325°F then toss the crab meat with the jack cheese.

2. Add the Worcestershire sauce, green onions, garlic, salt, lime juice, pepper, mustard, parmesan cheese, hot sauce and mayo into the meat mixture.

3. Combine the ingredients together until mixed then transfer into the oven.

4. Bake until done for 40 minutes then serve and enjoy as desired.

Nutrition Information

Calories: 519kcal | Fat: 43.1g | Carbohydrates: 6.8g | Protein: 32.4g

Mayo Pimento Cheese

Preparation Time: 10 minutes

Cook Time: 10 minutes

Servings: 10

Ingredients

1/4 teaspoon seasoning

1/2 cup mayonnaise

1 cup shredded sharp cheddar cheese

1 cup shredded Monterey Jack cheese

2 teaspoons shredded onion

3 tablespoons chopped pimentos

4 ounces' pack cream cheese

kosher salt & pepper, to taste

Instructions

1. Using a large mixing bowl, add in all the ingredients.

2. Use an electric mixer to combine the ingredients together until mixed

3. Serve and enjoy as desired.

Nutrition Information

Calories: 159kcal | Fat: 14.6g | Carbohydrates: 1.5g | Protein: 6.4g

Red Chuck Steak Curry

Preparation Time: 15 minutes

Cook Time: 4 hours

Servings: 4

Ingredients

1/4 cup beef broth

1/2 lemon juice & zest

1 teaspoon powdered turmeric

1 (14 ounce) can coconut cream

2 tablespoons Thai red curry paste

2 1/2 pounds cubed chuck steak

salt, to taste

Instructions

1. Heat the oven up to 210°F then use a large mixing bowl to combine the beef broth, salt, turmeric and curry paste together.

2. Pour in the lemon juice & zest then add in the steak, coconut cream and mix together until the meat is well coated.

3. Transfer the mixture into an oven proof dish, cover and bake in the oven for 2 hours then stir together and bake again uncovered for 1 1/2 hours until tenderized.

4. Once tenderized, take the dish out of the oven and pour into a mixing bowl and set aside.

5. Return the oven dish back into the oven and heat over 320 until the juices are reduced by half for 40 minutes.

6. Add the meat back into the reduced juices, stir together until coated then serve and enjoy as desired.

Nutrition Information

Calories: 656kcal | Fat: 32.9g | Carbohydrates: 1.3g | Protein: 82.7g

Mexican Crock Pot Beef Ribs

Preparation Time: 30 minutes

Cook Time: 7 1/2 hours

Servings: 8

Ingredients

1/2 cup water

1 cup chopped cilantro

1 teaspoon powdered chipotle

2 teaspoons paprika

2 teaspoons ground cumin

2 teaspoons ground turmeric

2 teaspoons ground coriander

3 1/2 pounds beef short ribs

4 minced garlic cloves

salt & pepper, to taste

Instructions

1. Using a small mixing bowl, add in all the dry ingredients and combine together.

2. Generously coat each of the short ribs with the spice mixture then place in a crock pot.

3. Top the coated ribs with the minced garlic and chopped cilantro then pour in the water.

4. Cook until tenderized for 6-7 hours over low settings to desired doneness.

5. Remove the meat from the pot then reduce the juices by half for 15 minutes over low heat.

6. Return the meat into the pot, shred and mix together until coated with the juices.

7. Serve and enjoy as desired.

Nutrition Information

Calories: 656kcal | Fat: 48.5g | Carbohydrates: 1.4g | Protein: 50.2g

Herbal Bacon Crisp

Preparation Time: 7 minutes

Cook Time: 12 minutes

Servings: 4

Ingredients

1/4 cup chopped basil

1/4 cup chopped parsley

3/4 pounds trimmed green beans

1 minced garlic clove

1 tablespoon olive oil

3 chopped bacon strips

salt, to taste

Instructions

1. Steam the green beans for 4 minutes until tenderized.

2. In the meantime, fry the chopped bacon strips until crispy and browned then take off the heat.

3. Drain the steamed beans then run under cold water.

4. Add all the ingredients into a large mixing bowl and combine everything together.

5. Serve and enjoy as desired.

Nutrition Information

Calories: 63kcal | Fat: 3.7g | Carbohydrates: 7.4g | Protein: 2g

Chicken Bacon Casserole

Preparation Time: 10 minutes

Cook Time: 20 minutes

Servings: 8

Ingredients

1/4 cup chicken stock

1 cup heavy cream

1 minced garlic clove

1 cup shredded cheddar cheese

4 chopped & seeded jalapeno peppers

5 bacon slices

6 chicken breasts

8 ounces' cream cheese

Instructions

1. Heat the oven up to 375°F then roast the bacon until golden brown & crispy then crumble and set aside.

2. Boil the chicken breast until tenderized then shred.

3. Using a large mixing bowl, add in the cream cheese, garlic, heavy cream & chicken stock together then season with salt & pepper to taste.

4. Arrange the shredded chicken at the bottom of a casserole dish then top with the heavy cream mixture and a garnish of the jalapeno.

5. Add in the baked bacon & cheddar cheese then bake for 20 minutes until set.

6. Check for desired doneness then serve and enjoy as desired.

Nutrition Information

Calories: 286kcal | Fat 24.8g | Carbohydrate 3.3g | Protein 12.5g

Keto Green Beans

Preparation Time: 2 minutes

Cook Time: 45 minutes

Servings: 14

Ingredients

1/4 teaspoon diced onion

1 tablespoon butter

1 tablespoon Italian dressing

2 tablespoons vegetable oil

4 (14.5 ounces cans) cut green beans

salt, to taste

garlic salt & pepper, to taste

Instructions

1. Pour all the ingredients (except the salt) into a large pan then bring to a boil over medium high heat.

2. Boil for 35-45 minutes until all of the juices are evaporated, occasionally stirring.

3. Season with the salt to taste then serve and enjoy.

Nutrition Information

Calories: 48kcal | Fat: 3.1g | Carbohydrates: 3.3g | Protein: 1g

BREAKFAST & BRUCH RECIPES

Ketogenic Muffin Cornbread

Preparation Time: 10 minutes

Cook Time: 15 minutes

Servings: 12

Ingredients

1/3 teaspoon salt

3/4 cup grated cheddar cheese

1 teaspoon baking powder

1.25 cups almond flour

3 large eggs

4 tablespoons melted butter

Instructions

1. Heat the oven up to 400°F then line a muffin pan with 8 liners and spray with cooking oil spray.

2. Add all the dry ingredients into a large mixing bowl and mix together.

3. Pour the wet ingredients into a separate bowl and combine then incorporate together with the dry ingredients mixture until mixed.

4. Scoop the batter into the prepared muffin pan then place inside the heated oven and bake until golden brown for 15 minutes.

5. Serve and enjoy as desired or store for up to a week.

Nutrition Information

Calories: 224kcal | Fat: 20g | Carbohydrates: 3.6g | Protein: 8.7g

Simple Cheesy Lasagna

Preparation Time: 30 minutes

Cook Time: 40 minutes

Servings: 4

Ingredients

for the cheeses

1/4 teaspoon Italian seasoning

1/4 cup shredded parmesan cheese

1/4 teaspoon powdered garlic & onion

1 1/4 cup shredded mozzarella cheese

2 large eggs

4 ounces softened cream cheese

for the filling

3/4 cup shredded mozzarella cheese

1-pound ground beef

1 teaspoon dried basil

1 teaspoon dried oregano

1 teaspoon powdered garlic

1 teaspoon Italian seasoning

1 tablespoon minced onion flakes

1 1/2 cups divided marinara sauce

6 tablespoons whole milk ricotta cheese

Instructions

1. Heat the oven up to 375°F then use a large parchment paper to prepare a baking dish.

2. Add the eggs and cream cheese into a large mixing bowl and whisk together until combined.

3. Add in the parmesan cheese, powdered garlic & onion, Italian seasoning and mix until incorporated.

4. Add the mozzarella cheese into the mixture, fold and combine then transfer the mixture into the prepared baking dish and spread out into an even layer.

5. bake the lasagna for 20-25 minutes set then cool, slice into thirds and place in the refrigerator.

6. With a large skillet, add in the ground beef, oregano, diced onion, basil, garlic powder, salt, combine and cook over medium high heat until the beef is browned.

7. Drain out the excess fat then pour in 3/4 cup of the sauce and simmer over low heat for 10 minutes.

8. Layer the bottom of a loaf pan with the remaining marinara sauce then add in a layer of the refrigerated cheese mix.

9. Add 1/3 of the beef mixture then 1/4 cup of the mozzarella cheese, 1/2 of the ricotta cheese and another layer of the cream cheese mixture.

10. Repeat the same process until all the ingredients are used up then garnish with the Italian seasoning and bake for 20 minutes.

11. Check for desired doneness, serve and enjoy.

Nutrition Information

Calories: 486 | Fat: 34g | Carbohydrates: 9.5g | Protein: 57g

Creamy Swedish Meatballs

Preparation Time: 15 minutes

Cook Time: 35 minutes

Servings: 20

Ingredients

for the meatballs

1/2 cup diced onion

1/2 teaspoon nutmeg

1/2 teaspoon allspice

1 large egg

1 teaspoon dried parsley

1 teaspoon powdered onion

1 teaspoon powdered garlic

1 tablespoon coconut flour

2 pounds ground beef

2 tablespoons vegetable oil

salt & black pepper, to taste

for the sauce

1 cup coconut cream

1 tablespoon gelatin

1 tablespoon Dijon mustard

1 tablespoon coconut flour

1 1/2 cups bone broth

2 thyme sprigs

2" piece lime peel

2 tablespoons coconut aminos

3 tablespoons melted butter

a dash of fish sauce

Instructions

1. Using a large skillet heat over medium low heat.

2. Add all the meatballs ingredients into a large mixing bowl and combine then mold into 20 even sized meatballs.

3. Pour the coconut oil into the skillet and heat until hot.

4. Add the meatballs into the skillet and fry until browned for 15 minutes, flipping as many times as possible to avoid burning.

5. Cook in batches and repeat the same process until all the ingredients are exhausted.

6. Transfer the cooked balls out onto a wire rack to drain and cool, covering with a large foil.

7. Add the butter into the skillet then pour in the coconut flour and stir cook until toasted and slightly browned.

8. Bloom the gelatin with the bone broth then pour into the skillet, whisk cooking until combined.

9. Pour in the fish sauce, mustard, coconut aminos, thyme and lime peel then simmer until reduced by 1/2 for 18 minutes.

10. Pour in the coconut cream, stir and allow to simmer until thickened then add in the meatballs and simmer until well coated with the sauce.

11. Serve and enjoy as desired.

Nutrition Information

Calories: 467kcal | Fat: 32g | Carbohydrates: 6g | Protein: 32g

Zucchini Bake Casserole

Preparation Time: 15 minutes

Cook Time: 45 minutes

Servings: 10

Ingredients

1/4 cup shredded parmesan cheese

1/2 cup diced onion

1/2 cup heavy cream

1 dash hot sauce

1 teaspoon Worcestershire sauce

2 pounds chopped zucchini

2 tablespoons fine dry bread crumbs

3 large eggs

4 tablespoons melted butter

salt & pepper, to taste

Instructions

1. Heat the oven up for 350°F

2. Add the zucchini & butter into large saucepan then cook, occasionally stirring over low heat until tenderized for 5 minutes.

3. Take the pan off the heat then set aside.

4. With a small mixing bowl, combine the eggs and heavy cream together.

5. Add the bread crumbs, Worcestershire sauce, onion, hot sauce, salt & pepper & 2 tablespoons parmesan cheese into the eggs mixture and combine together.

6. Add the mixture into the tenderized zucchini and mix until combined.

7. Butter coat a large casserole then pour in the zucchini mixture, top with the remaining cheese and bake uncovered for 35-40 minutes.

8. Serve and enjoy.

Nutrition Information

Calories: 137kcal | Fat: 12g | Carbohydrates: 5.4g | Protein: 3.9g

Bacon Artichokes with Mayo Dip

Preparation Time: 25 minutes

Cook Time: 40 minutes

Servings: 4

Ingredients

1/4 cup sour cream

1 cup mayonnaise

1 1/2 tablespoons chopped fresh rosemary

2 halved limes

4 bacon strips

6 trimmed medium fresh artichokes

8 cups water

Instructions

1. Pour the water and limes into a large Dutch oven and combine then boil over medium high heat.

2. Add in 3 artichokes and boil for 7 minutes then remove and drain, repeat the same process with the remaining artichokes.

3. Allow the artichokes to cool off then vertically half, scrape and dispose the fuzzy choke and set aside.

4. With a small skillet, cook the bacon strips until crisp then crumble and reserve a tablespoon of the bacon fat.

5. With a medium mixing bowl, add in the crumbled bacon, mayonnaise, bacon fat, rosemary, mayonnaise and allow to chill.

6. Grease a grill rack with cooking oil spray and heat up to a medium high heat.

7. Arrange the artichokes cut side down on the heated grill and grill for 5 minutes on each side until tenderized.

8. Serve and enjoy with a garnish of rosemary sprigs and the mayonnaise dip.

Nutrition Information

Calories: 477kcal | Fat: 46g | Carbohydrates: 13.9g | Protein: 5g

Goat Cheese Shakshuka

Preparation Time: 10 minutes

Cook Time: 20 minutes

Servings: 5

Ingredients

1/4 cup vegetable oil

1/2 chopped green bell pepper

1/2 teaspoon red pepper flakes

1 teaspoon sea salt

1 tablespoon paprika

1 chopped jalapeño pepper

1 diced medium yellow onion

3 cups chopped collards greens

4 ounces' goat cheese

4 minced garlic cloves

6 large eggs

28 ounces can crushed tomatoes

Instructions

1. Heat the oven up to 425°F then pour the vegetable oil in a large oven skillet and heat up over medium heat.

2. Add in the garlic, jalapeno, onion, bell pepper and sauté until tenderized for 4 minutes.

3. Pour the spices into the skillet and cook for 30 extra seconds until fragrant.

4. Pour the tomatoes and collard greens into the skillet and cook for 5 minutes until the greens are wilted.

5. Create a space in the middle of the sauce then break the egg into the middle then place the skillet inside the oven and cook until the egg whites are set for 5-10 minutes.

6. Serve, topped with the crumbled goat cheese and enjoy or refrigerate for later.

Nutritional Information

Calories: 248kcal | Fat: 18.5g | Protein: 12.1g | Carbohydrates: 10.1g

Keto Coconut Pancakes

Preparation Time: 12 minutes

Cook Time: 15 minutes

Servings: 3

Ingredients

1/4 teaspoon Himalayan salt

1/2 cup coconut flour

1/2 cup coconut cream

1/2 teaspoon baking soda

1/2 teaspoon Ceylon cinnamon

1/2 cup unsweetened almond milk

1 teaspoon vanilla

2 tablespoons coconut oil

4 large eggs

ghee, for frying

Instructions

1. Using a high speed blender, add in all the ingredients (except the ghee) then process until incorporated.

2. Pour the ghee into medium skillet and heat over medium heat then add in half of the batter and cook until golden then flip over and fry until golden.

3. Repeat the same process with the remaining batter until exhausted.

4. Serve and enjoy with any topping of choice.

Nutrition Information

Calories: 244kcal | Fat: 23g | Carbohydrates: 4.9g | Protein: 5.5g

Cinnamon Crunchy Toast Cereal

Preparation Time: 20 minutes

Cook Time: 15 minutes

Servings: 10

Ingredients

1/4 teaspoon kosher salt

1/2 teaspoon baking soda

1/2 teaspoon xanthan gum

1 large egg

2 teaspoons ground cinnamon

80g grass-fed butter

96g golden erythritol

192g almond flour

for the topping

2 tablespoons swerve

2 teaspoons ground cinnamon

28g grass-fed butter

Instructions

1. Using a medium mixing bowl, add in the almond flour, xanthan gum, cinnamon, salt and baking soda then whisk together until combined and set aside.

2. Using an electric mixer, beat the butter for 2 minutes then pour in the sweetener and beat until light and fluffy and the sweetener dissolved.

3. Pour in the egg and beat again until incorporated then add 1/2 of the flour mixture and whisk then pour in the remaining and incorporate together.

4. Use a cling film to tightly wrap the dough then refrigerate for an hour.

5. Heat the oven up to 350°F then roll the dough out between two parchment paper until thin then vertically cut out and slice crosswise into squares making slight holes in each with a fork.

6. Place the cinnamon toast crunch in a baking sheet and freeze for 15 minutes before baking.

7. Bake in the oven until golden for 10 minutes' coat with butter, sugar and allow to cool of completely.

8. Serve and enjoy or refrigerate for later.

Nutrition Information

Calories 172kcal | Fat: 16g | Carbohydrates: 4g | Protein: 4g

French Coconut Toast

Preparation Time: 30 minutes

Cook Time: 20 minutes

Servings: 3

Ingredients

1/3 cup coconut yogurt

1 tablespoon butter

1 loaf coconut bread

1 teaspoon vanilla extract

2 teaspoons stevia

to garnish

cacao nibs

organic berries

shredded coconut

Instructions

1. Slice the coconut bread into 3 pieces then vertically half each of the pieces.

2. Add the butter into a fry pan and heat until hot over medium heat.

3. Once hot, add 2 pieces of the bread into the pan and cook until toasted and golden on each side.

4. In the meantime, combine the vanilla, sweetener and coconut yogurt together, whisking until thicken.

5. Add the yogurt mix on of the toasted bread then top with the garnish ingredients cover with another toasted bread and set aside.

6. Repeat the same process with the remaining bread and ingredients then serve and enjoy.

Nutrition Information

Calories: 683kcal | Fat: 58g | Carbohydrates: 17g | Protein: 27.9g

Chocolate Cauliflower Oatmeal

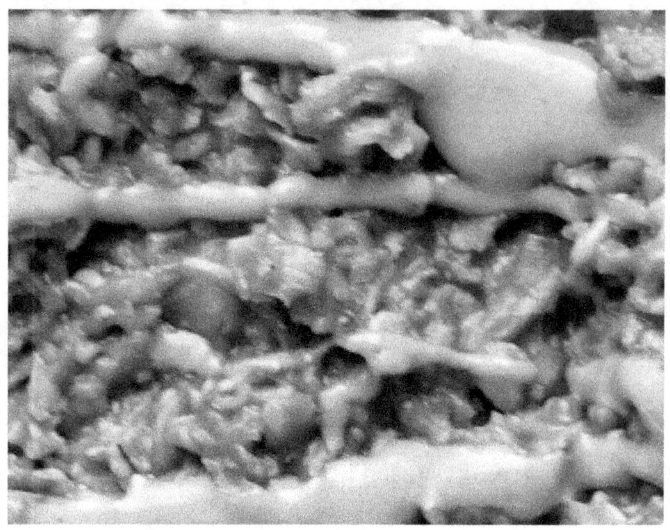

Preparation Time: 5 minutes

Cook Time: 10 minutes

Servings: 2

Ingredients

1/4 teaspoon salt

1 teaspoon stevia

1 scoop mito sweet

1 cup coconut milk

1 scoop collagen peptides

1 medium cauliflower head

1 tablespoon vegetable oil

1 1/2 tablespoons powdered cacao

4 beaten eggs

to garnish

cacao nibs

seasonal berries

Instructions

1. Chop the cauliflower head into florets and process until a rice like texture is achieved.

2. Using a medium sized saucepan, add in the coconut milk and simmer.

3. Pour in the cauliflower rice and stir with the milk, simmering over low heat for 4 minutes until thickened.

4. Fold the beaten eggs into the pan then add in the stevia, salt, mito sweet, collagen powder and powdered cacao.

5. Stir the mixture together and allow the eggs to cook through.

6. Serve warm with a garnish of the berries & cacao nibs and enjoy.

Nutrition Information

Calories: 464.9kcal | Fat: 41.2g | Carbohydrates: 18g | Protein: 22.1g

Baked Brussel Sprouts

Preparation Time: 5 minutes

Cook Time: 45 minutes

Servings: 4

Ingredients

1 pound halved Brussels sprouts

2 teaspoons turmeric

2 teaspoons sea salt

2 tablespoons butter

Instructions

1. Heat the oven up to 300°F.

2. Place the sprouts into a large baking pan then add in the butter and toss until well coated.

3. Season the sprouts with the turmeric & salt then place the pan in the oven and bake for 30-45 minutes.

4. Serve and enjoy as desired.

Nutrition Information

Calories: 104kcal | Fat: 5.9g | Carbohydrates: 11g | Protein: 4g

Bacon Loaded Cauliflower Bake

Preparation Time: 5 minutes

Cook Time: 8 minutes

Servings: 4

Ingredients

1/4 teaspoon chili powder

1/4 cup grated Parmesan cheese

1/4 teaspoon dry mustard powder

1/2 tablespoon butter

3/4 cup shredded cheddar cheese

1 minced garlic clove

1 tablespoon sour cream

1 chopped large cauliflower head

1 1/2 cups chicken broth

2 diced green onions, to top

4 crispy cooked bacon slices

salt & ground pepper, to taste

Instructions

1. Heat the oven up to 375°F then pour the broth into the insert of your Instant pot.

2. Fix the steamer into the instant pot then pour the cauliflower florets into the steamer basket.

3. Close the pot and set the valve to sealing then cook on manual setting for 3 minutes at high pressure.

4. Pull a quick release then drain the cauliflower and transfer into a high speed blender.

5. Add in the sour cream, butter, garlic, chili powder, mustard, pepper and salt then process until creamy & blended.

6. Pour the mixture out into a baking dish then top with the cheeses & bacon slices then bake until the cheese is melted for 5 minutes.

7. Serve and enjoy with a garnish of green onions.

Nutrition Information

Calories 235kcal | Fat: 19g | Carbohydrates 1g | Protein 12g

SALAD & SIDE RECIPES

Simple Ketogenic Coleslaw

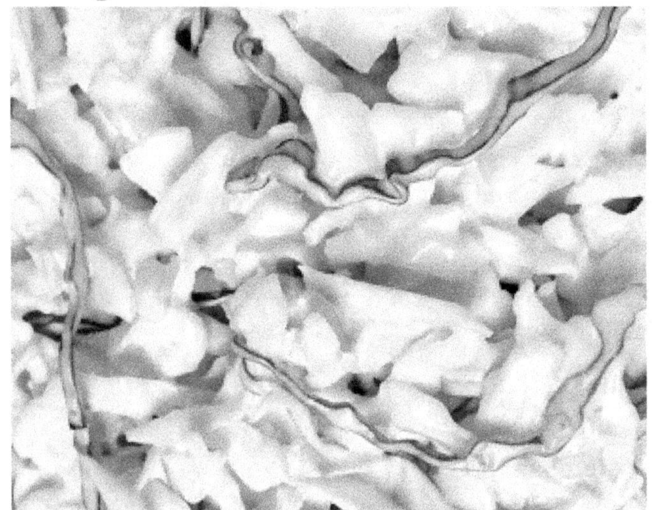

Preparation Time: 10 minutes

Cook Time: 0 minute

Servings: 6

Ingredients

1/2 cup mayonnaise

1/2 teaspoon celery seed, if desired

1 diced carrot

1 tablespoon swerve

1 chopped cabbage head

1 teaspoon Dijon mustard

1 tablespoon juiced lime

1 tablespoon apple cider vinegar

salt & pepper, to taste

Instructions

1. Combine the chopped cabbage and diced carrots into a mixing bowl and set aside.

2. With another mixing bowl, add in the vinegar, mayonnaise, mustard, lime juice, swerve, celery seed, salt, pepper and combine together until the swerve is dissolved.

3. Pour the vinegar mixture over the cabbage and carrots and toss together until well coated.

4. Serve as desired and enjoy.

Nutrition Information

Calories: 178kcal | Fat: 14g | Carbohydrates: 13g | Protein: 3g

Super Simple Salad

Preparation Time: 15 minutes

Cook Time: 0 minute

Servings: 3

Ingredients

1/2 cup vegetable oil

1/2 cup cider vinegar

1/2 cup cherries, dried

1/2 cup sunflower kernels

3 cups broccoli florets

5 tablespoons maple syrup

8 cups chopped kale

salt & pepper, to taste

Instructions

1. Using a large mixing bowl, add in the dried cherries, kernels, broccoli, kale and set aside.

2. Using a small mixing bowl, add in the maple syrup, vinegar, oil, salt, pepper and combine until mixed.

3. Cover the salad mixture with the syrup mix until fully coated.

4. Serve and enjoy or refrigerate for later.

Nutrition Information

Calories: 678kcal | Fat: 51.5g | Carbohydrates: 49.1g | Protein: 14.2g

Simple Fudge Pops

Preparation Time: 10 minute

Cook Time: 0 minute

Servings: 4

Ingredients

a pinch of salt

1 cup coconut cream

1 teaspoon vanilla powder

1 tablespoon cacao butter

1 tablespoon chocolate powder

2 large egg yolks

2 tablespoons coconut oil

2 tablespoons collagelatin

liquid stevia, to taste

Instructions

1. Using a small saucepan, pour in the coconut oil, cacao butter, coconut cream, collagelatin, powdered chocolate, salt and vanilla.

2. Place the pan over low heat and heat until all the ingredients are melted and combined then take off the heat and allow to cool.

3. Pour the mixture into a high speed blender then add in the stevia, egg yolks and process until smooth and creamy.

4. Pour the mixture into 1ce block molds then freeze until set then serve with melted chocolate and enjoy.

Nutrition Information

Calories: 303kcal | Fat: 26g | Carbohydrates: 6g | Protein: 11g

Smokey Chicken Salad

Preparation Time: 10 minutes

Cook Time: 0 minute

Servings: 4

Ingredients

1/2 cup mayonnaise

1/2 teaspoon liquid smoke

1 tablespoon mustard

1 cooked & chopped rotisserie chicken

1 diced green onion

2 chopped celery stalks

for the seasonings

1 teaspoon powdered garlic

1 teaspoon powdered onion

1 teaspoon paprika

1 teaspoon monk fruit sweetener

1/2 teaspoon cayenne powder

salt & pepper, to taste

Instructions

1. Using a medium sized bowl, add in mayonnaise, liquid smoke, mustard and whisk together.

2. Combine all the seasonings ingredients together then pour into the mayonnaise mix and combine.

3. Add in the green onion, celery, chicken, toss together until coated with the mayo mixture.

4. Serve and enjoy as desired or refrigerate for later.

Nutrition Information

Calories: 257kcal | Fat: 18g | Carbohydrates: 2g | Protein: 21g

Bacon Fried Cabbage

Preparation Time: 10 minutes

Cook Time: 20 minutes

Servings: 3

Ingredients

1 chopped cabbage head

6 bacon strips

vegetable oil

salt & pepper, to taste

Instructions

1. Using a large skillet, pour in the vegetable oil and heat until hot over medium high heat.

2. Add the bacon strips into the hot oil and fry until crisp then transfer onto a paper towel to drain.

3. Reserve 2 tablespoons of the bacon grease in the skillet then add in the chopped cabbage and top with the crumbled bacon.

4. Cook the mixture for 5 minutes over medium high heat, occasionally stirring.

5. Reduce the heat to a low, cover and cook for 5 extra minutes until the cabbage is tenderized as desired.

6. Season with salt & pepper to taste then serve and enjoy.

Nutrition Information

Calories: 193kcal | Fat: 8.8g | Carbohydrates: 13.7g | Protein: 7g

Low Carb Chicken Salad

Preparation Time: 5 minutes

Cook Time: 20 minutes

Servings: 6

Ingredients

1/4 cup mayonnaise

1/4 cup toasted pecans

1/4 cup chopped celery

1/2 cup sour cream

1 tablespoon juiced lime

2 tablespoons chopped parsley

2 tablespoons diced green onions

3 cups cooked chicken breast

salt & pepper, to taste

Instructions

1. Chop the cooked chicken into small chunks and set aside.

2. Using a small mixing bowl add in the celery, parsley, onions, pecans, mayonnaise, juiced lime, salt & pepper, sour cream and combine together.

3. Toss the chicken chunks with the cream mixture, season with extra salt & pepper if desired.

4. Serve and enjoy.

Nutrition Information

Calories: 325kcal | Fat: 25g | Carbohydrates: 2g | Protein: 23g

SNACKS & PIE RECIPES

Vanilla Pecan Pie

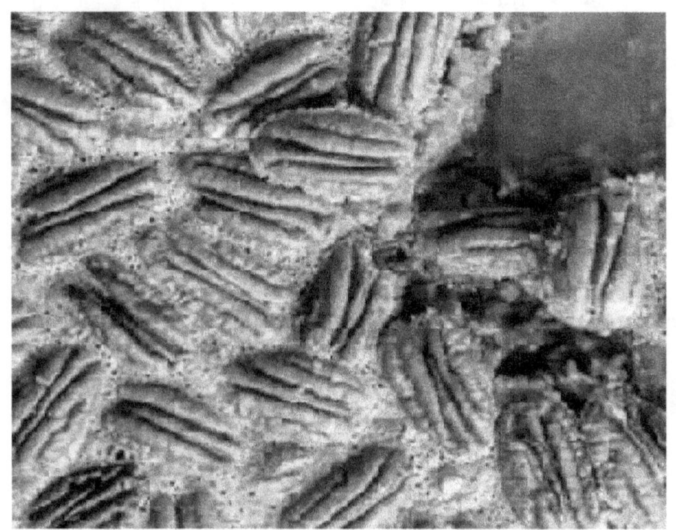

Preparation Time: 25 minutes

Cook Time: 1 hour 5 minutes

Servings: 10 slices

Ingredients

for the crust

3/4 cup almond flour

3/4 tablespoon olive oil

3/4 teaspoon vanilla extract

1 1/2 large eggs

3 tablespoons erythritol

6 tablespoons butter

pink Himalayan salt, to taste

for the filing

1 teaspoon vanilla extract

1 1/2 cups chopped raw pecans

2 large eggs

2 tablespoons butter

10 tablespoons erythritol

10 tablespoons maple syrup

Instructions

for the crust

1. Add all the dry ingredients into a mixing bowl and incorporate then set aside.

2. Add the wet ingredients into another bowl and mix then pour in the dry ingredients mixture and combine together until a soft dough is formed.

3. Grease a fry pan with cooking oil spray then add in the soft dough and press into the bottom and side of the pan.

4. Bake in the oven for 12 minutes at 350°F ensuring the edges don't burn then take out of the oven and allow to cool off.

5. Add all the filling ingredients (except the pecans) into a mixing bowl and combine together.

6. Arrange the bottom of the cooled crust with the chopped pecans then cover with the extract mixture and bake for 50 minutes at 350°F.

7. Allow the pie to cool off then slice, serve and enjoy.

Nutrition Information

Calories: 259.2kcal | Fat: 25g | Carbohydrates: 9.3g | Protein: 4.65g

Creamy Pecan Pie

Preparation Time: 1 hour

Cook Time: 1 hour

Servings: 10 slices

Ingredients

1 sweet pie crust

for the filling

1/2 cup erythritol

3/4 cup butter, unsalted

1 large egg

1 1/2 cups chopped raw pecans

1 1/2 teaspoon powdered beef gelatin

1 3/4 cup heavy whipping cream

15 drops liquid stevia

pink Himalayan salt, to taste

Instructions

1. Bake the pie crust in the oven for 10 minutes at 350°F then set aside to cool.

2. Using a large saucepan, add in the erythritol, butter and melt for 5 minutes over medium low heat.

3. Gently add in 1 1/2 cups of the cream and allow to simmer until thickened for 15-20 minutes then take of the heat.

4. Pour the stevia and vanilla extract into the simmered cream mix and stir in then allow to cool.

5. Add the gelatin powder into the remaining cream and allow to bloom for 5 minutes then break the egg and whisk in a separate mixing bowl.

6. Gently drizzle in 1/4 cup of the cream sauce, whisking to temper the egg then pour in the remaining sauce and whisk with the bloomed gelatin.

7. Arrange the chopped pecans at the bottom of the cooled crust then cover with the cream sauce mixture and cover the edges with a foil.

8. Bake in the oven until the filling is set for 45-55 minutes then set aside to cool off.

9. Slice into pieces, serve and enjoy or store for later.

Nutrition Information

Calories: 505kcal | Fat: 51g | Carbohydrates: 7g | Protein 7g

Ketogenic Butter Cake

Preparation Time: 10 minutes

Cook Time: 45 minutes

Servings: 16

Ingredients

1/4 cup egg white protein

1/2 cup heavy whipping cream

1 cup water

1 cup swerve

1 tablespoon baking powder

1 cup melted butter, salted

1 cup coconut flour, with extra

2 1/2 cups almond flour

3 teaspoons vanilla extract

7 large eggs

salt, to taste

Instructions

1. Using an electric mixer, beat the swerve and melted butter together until fluffy.

2. Add the wet ingredients into the swerve mix and stir then pour in the dry ingredients and mix until thick and combined.

3. Coat a fry pan with cooking oil spray then dust with some coconut flour and add in the cake dough.

4. Bake the cake until golden brown for 45-50 minutes at 350°F then check for doneness as desired.

5. Allow the cake to cool off then slice, serve and enjoy.

Nutrition Information

Calories: 267kcal | Fat: 25g | Carbohydrates: 7.1g | Protein: 8.2g

Golden Keto Biscuits

Preparation Time: 5 minutes

Cook Time: 10 minutes

Servings: 12

Ingredients

1/2 cup sour cream

1/2 teaspoon powdered onion

1/2 teaspoon powdered garlic

1/2 cup grated parmesan cheese

1 tablespoon baking powder

1 1/2 cups almond flour

2 large eggs

4 tablespoons melted butter

salt, to taste

Instructions

1. Heat the oven up to 450°F then combine all the dry ingredients together until mixed.

2. Separately mix the wet ingredients together then combine with the dry ingredients until incorporated.

3. Grease the baking pan with cooking oil spray then drop the biscuit batter in dollops onto the pan.

4. Place the pan into the oven and cook for 10-13 minutes until golden.

5. Serve and enjoy.

Nutrition Information

Calories: 164kcal | Fat: 14.6g | Carbohydrates: 4.6g | Protein: 5.9g

Cacao & Coconut Donuts

Preparation Time: 4 minutes

Cook Time: 8 minutes

Servings: 5

Ingredients

for the donuts

1/2 cup sifted banana flour

1 teaspoon baking powder

1 tablespoon melted butter

1 teaspoon apple cider vinegar

1 tablespoon sifted powdered cacao

2 large eggs

2 teaspoons vanilla extract

3 teaspoons Ceylon cinnamon

3 tablespoons granulated sweetener

4 tablespoons coconut milk

a pinch of salt

cooking spray oil

for the icing top

1/4 chopped avocado

1 1/2 teaspoons powdered cacao powder

4 tablespoons coconut cream

stevia drops, to taste

a dash of vanilla extract

to garnish

shredded coconut

a handful cacao nibs

Instructions

1. Heat the oven up to 350°F then grease a baking tray with the cooking oil spray.

2. Using a medium mixing bowl, add in all the donut ingredients and combine together.

3. Transfer the batter mixture into donut molds, filling each up to 3/4 full.

4. Bake the donut for 8 minutes until cooked through.

5. Then the pan out of the oven then transfer the baked donuts onto a cooling rack.

6. Add all the icing ingredients into a mixing bowl and combine together.

7. Top the donuts with the icing mix and garnish with the shredded coconut & cacao nibs.

8. Serve and enjoy warm.

Nutrition Information

Calories: 112kcal | Fat: 6.6g | Carbohydrates: 13.6g | Protein: 3g

Keto Glazed Cinnamon Rolls

Preparation Time: 20 minutes

Cook Time: 25 minutes

Servings: 10

Ingredients

1 batch of chilled caramel sauce

for the cinnamon

1 tablespoon apple cider vinegar

1 1/2 teaspoons baking powder

2 tablespoons ghee

2 cups macadamia nuts

2 teaspoons vanilla extract

2 tablespoons ground psyllium husks

3 teaspoons Ceylon cinnamon

3 tablespoons sweetened erythritol

4 large eggs

8 tablespoons coconut flour

a pinch of salt

for the glaze

2 teaspoons erythritol

2 tablespoon melted ghee

4 tablespoons coconut cream

Instructions

1. Using a high speed blender, add in the macadamia nuts and blend into a fine texture then combine all the cinnamon ingredients together and refrigerate for an hour.

2. Heat the oven up to 350°F then prepare a baking tray with a large parchment paper.

3. Mold the cinnamon mixture into a rectangle and coat with the caramel sauce then roll the dough into logs and seal the edges.

4. Slice the log into 10 rolls then transfer onto the lined baking tray and bake until done for 25 minutes.

5. In the meantime, combine all the glaze ingredients together then drizzle over the baked rolls until covered.

6. Serve warm and enjoy or refrigerate for later.

Nutrition Information

Calories: 477kcal | Fat: 45.6g | Carbohydrates: 17.1g | Protein: 5.6g

Almond Cacao Butter Crepes

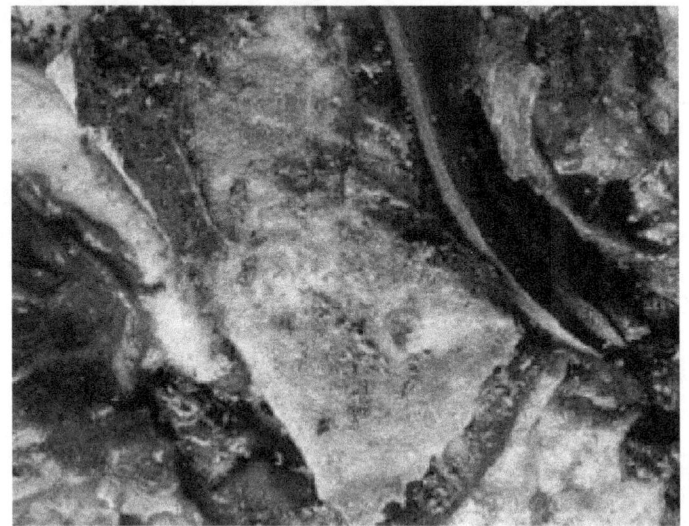

Preparation Time: 5 minutes

Cook Time: 20 minutes

Servings: 8

Ingredients

for the crepes

1/4 teaspoon sea salt

1/2 cup almond milk

1/2 teaspoon vanilla extract

3 tablespoons coconut flour

3 teaspoons powdered arrowroot

4 tablespoons coconut oil

6 medium size eggs

ghee, to grease

for the butter spread

1 teaspoon powdered cacao

4 tablespoons almond butter

6 tablespoons coconut milk

a pinch sea salt

Instructions

1. Using a large mixing bowl, add in all the creeps ingredients and mix together until smooth and blended then allow to sit for 5 minutes.

2. Grease a large skillet with the ghee then place over medium heat and heat up until hot.

3. Reduce the heat to a medium low then add in 1/4 cup of the batter into the skillet, swirl around then cook until the edges begin to crisp for a minute.

4. Flip the creeps oven then cook for another 30 seconds before transferring onto a cooling rack to drain then repeat the same process with the remaining batter.

5. Combine all the butter spread mixture together until smooth and cream.

6. Serve and enjoy the crepes with a spread of the butter mixture.

Nutrition Information

Calories: 217kcal | Fat: 20.6g | Carbohydrates: 4g | Protein: 6g

Simple Fluffy Buns

Preparation Time: 20 minutes

Cook Time: 40 minutes

Servings: 4

Ingredients

1/4 cup coconut flour

1/2 tablespoon apple cider vinegar

1 cup water

1 teaspoon dried thyme

1 teaspoon baking powder

1 teaspoon dried oregano

2 egg yolks

2 tablespoons ground psyllium husks

4 egg whites

salt & pepper, to taste

Instructions

1. Heat the oven up to 350°F then use a large parchment paper to prepare a baking sheet.

2. Beat the egg whites with a whisker until a stiff peak is formed then set aside.

3. Add the remaining ingredients into a separate bowl and combine then fold in the whisked egg whites.

4. Divide the batter into thick even rolls then arrange on the prepared baking sheet.

5. Place the baking sheet in the oven and bake until cooked through for 40 minutes.

6. Serve warm and enjoy.

Nutrition Information

Calories: 120kcal | Fat: 3.1g | Carbohydrates: 23.4g | Protein: 6g

Herbal Focaccia Bread

Preparation Time: 10 minutes

Cook Time: 20 minutes

Servings: 8

Ingredients

for the flour

1/4 cup coconut flour

1/2 teaspoon xanthan gum

1/2 teaspoon baking soda

1/2 teaspoon baking powder

1 teaspoon salt

1 cup almond flour

1 teaspoon powdered garlic

for the eggs

1 tablespoon juiced lime

2 large eggs

2 teaspoon vegetable oil, with extra to drizzle

Instructions

1. Heat the oven up to 350°F then prepare a baking tray with a large parchment paper.

2. Combine all the flour ingredients together, ensuring that there are ni lumps.

3. Combine the egg ingredients together then pour into the flour mixture and incorporate.

4. Transfer the mixture onto the baking tray then use a wet spatula to smoothen the top and edges.

5. Create shallow dimples into the dough then place in the oven and bake for 10 minutes.

6. Drizzle the top of the focaccia with oil then bake until browned for an extra 10 minutes.

7. Allow the bread to cool off then slice, serve and enjoy.

Nutrition Information

Calories 166kcal | Fat: 13g | Carbohydrates: 7g | Protein: 7g

Simple Oreos

Preparation Time: 15 minutes

Cook Time: 30 minutes

Servings: 10

Ingredients

for the cookies

1/4 cup powder cacao

1/2 teaspoon baking soda

1 large egg

1 teaspoon vanilla extract

1 teaspoon apple cider vinegar

1 1/2 cups blanched almond meal

3 tablespoons coconut oil

4 tablespoons erythritol

a pinch of salt

for the cream filling

1/2 cup of soaked cashews

1 teaspoon vanilla extract

2 tablespoons erythritol

3 tablespoons coconut oil

3 tablespoons cacao butter

Instructions

1. Heat the oven up to 350°F then prepare a baking sheet with parchment paper.

2. Add all the cookies ingredients into a mixing bowl and combine together, adjusting the sweetener to taste.

3. Use a rolling pin to roll the dough out on a flat work station then cut out 20 round shaped bites from the dough.

4. Arrange the cut dough on the prepared baking sheet then bake in the oven for 15 minutes.

5. In the meantime, add all the filling ingredients into a high speed blender then pulse until smooth and combined.

6. Add a teaspoon of the filling cream on each of the cooled cookies, then spread out to edges and top with another cookie.

7. Repeat the same process with the remaining cookies and fillings then serve and enjoy.

Nutrition Information

Calories: 269kcal | Fat: 25g | Carbohydrates: 13g | Protein: 6g

Chocolate Lava Cake

Preparation Time: 5 minutes

Cook Time: 15 minutes

Servings: 4

Ingredients

1/8 cup chocolate chunks

1 tablespoon erythritol

1 tablespoon almond flour

1 teaspoon vanilla extract

2 large eggs

2 ounces' chocolate

2 tablespoons powdered erythritol

2 ounces' ghee, with extra to grease

sea salt, to taste

to garnish

almond butter

fresh raspberries

Instructions

1. Heat the oven up to 350°F then coat two ramekins with the extra ghee.

2. Place a small saucepan over low heat add in the ghee, 2 ounces of chocolate and melt until combined.

3. Pour the vanilla, beaten eggs & salt into a small mixing bowl then whisk together until frothy.

4. Combine the chocolate and vanilla mixture together then add in the flour, sweetener and combine together.

5. Fill the greased ramekins halfway with the batter then add in the chocolate chunks and top with the remaining batter.

6. Bake in the oven until the tops are set and but jiggly for 9 minutes.

7. Allow the cakes to cool off then top with the almond butter, berries, serve and enjoy.

Nutrition Information

Calories: 559kcal | Fat: 52g | Carbohydrates: 27.9g | Protein: 9.7g

Ice Cream Cookie Sandwiches

Preparation Time: 15 minutes

Cook Time: 15 minutes

Servings: 5

Ingredients

for the cookies

1/3 cup chopped chocolate

1/2 teaspoon baking powder

1 large egg

1 teaspoon apple cider vinegar

2 cups almond flour

2 teaspoons vanilla extract

3 tablespoons melted butter

3 tablespoons collagen protein

salt, to taste

stevia, to taste

for the ice cream

1/4 cup cocoa powder

1/4 cup filtered water

1 teaspoon cinnamon, if desired

1 teaspoon apple cider vinegar

2 teaspoons vanilla extract

3 tablespoons coconut oil with extra

3 1/2 tablespoons stevia

3 1/2 tablespoons melted cacao butter

4 large eggs

4 large egg yolks

6 tablespoons vegetable oil with extra

7 tablespoons melted butter

Instructions

1. Heat the oven up to 340°F then use a large parchment paper to line two baking trays.

2. Using a large mixing bowl, combine the baking powder, collagen protein, salt and almond meal together.

3. Pour the vinegar on the baking powder and allow to fizzy then add in the remaining cookie ingredients and combine together.

4. Taste and adjust for sweetness then mold into 10 ball shapes and arrange over the baking tray.

5. Using a rolling pin, slightly press down on the dough until flatten then bake until golden brown for 15 minutes.

6. Remove the trays out of the oven and transfer the bakes onto a cooling rack.

7. In the meantime, add all the ice cream ingredients into a high speed blender then blitz for 2 minutes.

8. Taste and adjust for sweetener then pour into an ice cream machine and churn for 15-20 minutes.

9. Freeze the ice cream mixture for 15 minutes then spoon the freezed cream onto one of the cookies and top with another cookie.

10. Repeat the same process with the remaining cream and cookies then serve and enjoy.

Nutrition Information

Calories: 662kcal | Fat: 51g | Carbohydrates: 15g | Protein: 25g

Southern Dressed Ketogenic Cornbread

Preparation Time: 5 minutes

Cook Time: 35 minutes

Servings: 6

Ingredients

1/2 teaspoon salt

2 cups chicken broth

2 ounces chopped celery

2 teaspoons baking powder

2 tablespoons ground sage

2 1/2 cups almond flour

3 large eggs

3 ounces diced onion

4 tablespoons melted butter

cooking oil spray

Instructions

1. Heat the oven up to 350°F.

2. Using a large mixing bowl, add in the sage, salt, baking powder, almond flour and whisk together until mixed.

3. Add in the melted butter, eggs and whisk until combined then fold in the celery and onion.

4. Gently pour in the broth and whisk until mixed then coat a large baking dish with cooking oil spray.

5. Pour the batter mixture into the greased dish and bake until the top is browned for 35 minutes.

6. Allow the bread to cool off then slice, serve and enjoy.

Nutrition Information

Calories: 415kcal | Fat: 35g | Carbohydrates: 10.9g | Protein: 13.6g

Simple Ketogenic Collagen Bread

Preparation Time: 10 minutes

Cook Time: 1 hour 40 minutes

Servings: 10

Ingredients

1/2 cup collagen protein

1 teaspoon xanthan gum

1 tablespoon coconut oil

1 teaspoon baking powder

5 large eggs

6 tablespoons almond flour

a pinch of stevia

a pinch Himalayan pink salt

Instructions

1. Heat the oven up to 325°F then generously grease a large loaf pan with coconut oil.

2. Using a large mixing bowl, beat the egg whites until a stiff peak is reached then set aside.

3. With a small mixing bowl, add in the dry ingredients and combine together with a pinch of stevia then set aside.

4. Add the wet ingredients into a small mixing bowl and whisk together then pour into the egg whites, adding the dry ingredients mixture together mixing until thick and combined.

5. Transfer the batter into the prepared pan then place inside the oven and bake for 40 minutes.

6. Take the pan out of the oven then allow to cool off before slicing.

7. Serve and enjoy as desired.

Nutrition Information

Calories: 145kcal | Fat: 9.1g | Carbohydrates: 8.6g | Protein: 21.5g

Simple Steak Hamburger

Preparation Time: 15 minutes

Cook Time: 20 minutes

Servings: 4

Ingredients

1 cup beef broth

2 tablespoons olive oil

plain flour

ground beef

diced sweet onion

Instructions

1. Pour the oil into a large skillet then beat the form the beef into doughnut shaped patties.

2. Dredge the doughnut beef patties in the plain flour until fully covered then transfer into the oil in the skillet.

3. Turn the heat up to a medium and cook until browned on each side for a few minutes.

4. Add the diced onions into the skillet and stir cook until slightly browned.

5. Pour the beef broth into the skillet, cover and cook for 10 minutes until the beef is no longer pink in the middle.

6. Serve and enjoy.

Nutrition Information

Calories: 297kcal | Fat: 19.6g | Carbohydrates: 5g | Protein: 25.1g

VEGETABLE & SEAFOOD RECIPES

Oven Roasted Vegetables

Preparation Time: 10 minutes

Cook Time: 10 minutes

Servings: 3

Ingredients

3 cups assorted vegetables

vegetable oil

a handful of parsley

salt & black pepper, to taste

Instructions

1. Heat the oven up to 425°F then chop the vegetables and transfer into a rimmed baking sheet.

2. Drizzle the chopped veggies with the oil until well coated then season with salt, pepper and the parsley then toss until everything is well incorporated.

3. Place the baking sheet in the oven and bake for 10 minutes until the veggies are browned as desired.

4. Serve and enjoy.

Nutrition Information

Calories: 85kcal | Fat: 5g | Carbohydrates: 7.6g | Protein: 2.8g

Baked Okra Slices

Preparation Time: 5 minutes

Cook Time: 15 minutes

Servings: 3

Ingredients

1 tablespoon vegetable oil

18 stemmed fresh okra pods, chopped into 1/3" rounds

kosher salt & black pepper, to taste

Instructions

1. Heat the oven up to 425°F.

2. Line a large baking sheet with aluminum foil then arrange the okra in one layer on the sheet.

3. Drizzle the oil with salt & pepper then place the sheet in the oven and bake for 10-5 minutes until crispy and golden at the edges.

4. Serve and enjoy.

Nutrition Information

Calories: 436kcal | Fat: 6.8g | Carbohydrates: 77g | Protein: 28.4g

Braised Bacon Greens

Preparation Time: 5 minutes

Cook Time: 50 minutes

Servings: 3

Ingredients

1/2 pound chopped bacon

1 tablespoon balsamic vinegar

2 bay leaves

2 cups chicken stock

2 thinly sliced shallots

2 large bunches chopped of collard greens

5 minced garlic cloves

sea salt, to taste

Instructions

1. Place a large Dutch oven over medium heat then add in the chopped bacon pieces and cook until crispy.

2. Transfer the bacon pieces onto a paper towel to drain, leaving the fat in the oven.

3. Add the shallots and garlic into the Dutch oven and cook until browned and fragrant for 10 minutes.

4. Pour in the collard greens, vinegar, stock, salt, bay leaves, crumbled bacon and mix to combine.

5. Cover and allow to cook for 30 minutes then an extra 10 minutes uncovered for the liquid to reduce.

6. Serve and enjoy.

Nutrition Information

Calories: 413kcal | Fat: 30.3g | Carbohydrates: 19.9g | Protein: 18.3g

Bacon Fried Brussels Sprouts

Preparation Time: 5 minutes

Cook Time: 25 minutes

Servings: 4

Ingredients

1/2 pound chopped lean bacon

1 diced medium yellow onion

2 cups chicken broth

2 minced garlic cloves

2 pounds trimmed Brussels sprouts

4 tablespoons butter

salt & ground pepper, to taste

Instructions

1. Using a large pot placed over medium heat, add in the chopped bacon and fry until crisp then drain over paper towels.

2. Add the garlic and onion into the bacon fat and sauté for 3 minutes until tenderized.

3. Add in the Brussels sprouts and stir until coated in the bacon fat.

4. Season with salt & pepper to taste then pour in the broth and cook covered for 15 minutes until tenderized over low heat.

5. Add in the butter and stir until melted then transfer onto a serving platter, garnish with the chopped bacon, serve and enjoy.

Nutrition Information

Calories: 318kcal | Fat: 14.6g | Carbohydrates: 24.6g | Protein: 22.8g

Butter Roasted Chicken Vegetables

Preparation Time: 20 minutes

Cook Time: 1 hour 30 minutes

Servings: 5

Ingredients

1/2 cup butter

1/2 teaspoon powdered garlic

1 teaspoon basil

1 teaspoon paprika

1 teaspoon parsley

5 pounds' chicken fryer

chopped assorted vegetables

kosher salt & black pepper, to taste

Instructions

1. Heat the oven up to 425°F then coat a large baking pan with the butter.

2. With a small mixing bowl, add in all the seasonings and combine.

3. Generously coat the chicken fryer with extra butter then cover with the seasonings mixture, setting some aside for the vegetables.

4. Arrange the chopped vegetables around the covered chicken then sprinkle with the remaining seasoning mix.

5. Place the pan in the oven and bake for 1 1/2 hours, basting the chicken and veggies with extra butter at intervals.

6. Chicken is done once the juices run clear and cooked through.

7. Serve and enjoy as desired.

Nutrition Information

Calories: 619kcal | Fat: 23.9g | Carbohydrates: 6g | Protein: 104.5g

Southern Shrimp & Grits

Preparation Time: 10 minutes

Cook Time: 20 minutes

Servings: 4

Ingredients

for the shrimps

1 diced onion

1 green bell pepper

1 tablespoon seasoning

1-pound deveined shrimp

5 chopped bacon slices

for the cauliflower grits

1 cup shredded cheddar cheese

2 tablespoons butter

4 cups riced cauliflower

4 tablespoons minced garlic cloves

salt & pepper, to taste

Instructions

1. Using a medium skillet, fry the bacon over medium heat then crumble and reserve the bacon grease

2. Add the onion & pepper into the skillet and cook until translucent.

3. Return the bacon into the skillet with the shrimp, seasoning and cook until the shrimp is pink.

4. Prepare the cauliflower florets until tenderized then drain.

5. Add in the remaining grits ingredients and cook until combined.

6. Serve the grits, topped with bacon, shrimps and enjoyed.

Nutrition Information

Calories: 383kcal | Fat: 21g | Carbohydrates: 9g | Protein: 37g

Paleo Shrimp & Grits

Preparation Time: 15 minutes

Cook Time: 25 minutes

Servings: 4

Ingredients

for the shrimp

1/2 diced large onion

1 lime zest

1 tablespoon lime juice

1 teaspoon red pepper flakes

1 tablespoon white wine vinegar

1 tablespoon fresh oregano, chopped

2 bacon slices

2 tablespoons butter

2 divided teaspoons dried oregano

3 tablespoons vegetable oil

6 minced & divided garlic cloves

15 pieces shelled & deveined raw shrimp

salt & black pepper, to taste

for the cauliflower

1/4 cup almond milk

1/4 teaspoon cayenne pepper

1 tablespoon butter

1 large cauliflower head, chopped into florets

4 minced garlic cloves

salt & pepper, to taste

Instructions

1. Using a small mixing bowl, pour in the oil, a teaspoon of oregano, lime zest, minced garlic and combine together.

2. Place the shrimps in the oil mixture and allow to marinate for an hour.

3. Pour a 2 inches of water into a large pot and heat until boiling then fit in a steamer.

4. Pour the cauliflower florets into the pot, cover and steam until tenderized for 14 minutes then drain and return to the pot.

5. Pour the almond milk, butter and minced garlic into the cauliflower pot then blend with an immersion blender until thick and combined like a grits then sprinkle with salt & pepper as desired.

6. Using a large skillet, prepare the bacon over medium heat until crispy then remove the bacon and crumble, leaving the fat in the pot.

7. Add some butter into the skillet and heat to melt then pour in the diced onion and sauté until tenderized for 5 minutes.

8. Pour in the remaining garlic, pepper flakes, oregano and sauté, stirring occasionally for 1-2 minutes.

9. Pour in the wine vinegar and stir, add in the shrimp and cook for 5 minutes until cooked through.

10. Take the skillet off then heat, pour in the juiced lime and stir then season with the salt & pepper.

11. Serve the grits, topped with onions, shrimps, bacon slices garnished oregano and enjoy.

Nutrition Information

Calories: 279kcal | Fat: 21.6g | Carbohydrates: 13.3g | Protein: 8.2g

Fried Green Tomatoes

Preparation Time: 10 minutes

Cook Time: 10 minutes

Servings: 4

Ingredients

1/4 cup butter

1/2 teaspoon powdered garlic

1 large egg

1 cup almond flour

1 teaspoon powdered onion

2 tablespoons water

2 medium green tomatoes, chopped into 1/4" bits

black pepper, to taste

sea salt & cayenne pepper, to taste

Instructions

1. Season the chopped tomatoes with some salt then allow to rest for 5 minutes.

2. Using a small mixing bowl, combine the water and egg together.

3. Using a separate bowl, add in the powdered onion & garlic, cayenne powder, black pepper, salt, almond flour and combine together.

4. Add the butter into a large skillet and melt over medium high heat.

5. Dredge the seasoned tomatoes through the egg mixture then run through the flour mixture and shake off excesses.

6. Fry the slices in the butter until golden brown for 4 minutes per side.

7. Transfer the fried tomato slices onto a paper towel to drain then season with salt to taste.

Nutrition Information

Calories: 186kcal | Fat: 16.6g | Carbohydrates: 8g | Protein: 4.4g

Collard Green Soul Food

Preparation Time: 25 minutes

Cook Time: 1 hour

Servings: 3

Ingredients

1 tablespoon coconut oil

1 diced small white onion

1 teaspoon red pepper flakes

1 cooked large smoked turkey leg

3 cups chicken broth

3 minced garlic cloves

32 ounces chopped collard greens

hot sauce, as desired

salt & pepper, to taste

Instructions

1. Using a large skillet, pour in the oil and heat up over medium heat.

2. Add in the diced onions and sauté until tenderized.

3. Pour the minced garlic into the hot oil mix and cook until fragrant.

4. Pour in the prepared turkey leg, red pepper flakes, chicken broth and bring to a boil.

5. Reduce the heat and allow to slightly boil for 25 minutes.

6. Take the turkey leg out of the skillet and shred the meat from the bone.

7. Chop the turkey into pieces, skin and return back into the pot.

8. Simmer for 10 minutes then add in the collard greens, cover and simmer until a desired texture is achieved.

9. Season with salt & pepper to taste, serve and enjoy with a garnish of hot sauce.

Nutrition Information

Calories: 170kcal | Fat: 5.9g | Carbohydrates: 7.1g | Protein: 10.4g

Fried Okra Slices

Preparation Time: 10 minutes

Cook Time: 5 minutes

Servings: 5

Ingredients

1/3 cup almond flour

1-pound fresh okra

olive oil, to fry

salt & pepper, to taste

Instructions

1. Dice the okra into 1/4" slices then remove the stems.

2. Pout the oil into a large skillet and heat up on medium high heat.

3. Using a medium sized bowl, add in the almond flour and combine with the salt & pepper.

4. Add in the okra slices and toss until coated.

5. Transfer the coated okra into the heated oil, continually stirring until browned.

6. Transfer the fried okra slices onto a large paper towel to drain.

7. Once drained, serve and enjoy as desired.

Nutrition Information

Calories: 130kcal | Fat: 10g | Carbohydrates: 7g | Protein: 3g

Mayo & Mustard Crusted Ham

Preparation Time: 13 minutes

Cook Time: 15 minutes

Servings: 2

Ingredients

1/2 cup mayonnaise

1 smoked ham

1 cup prepared mustard

2 tablespoons minced garlic

2 tablespoons chopped rosemary

freshly ground pepper

Instructions

1. Add all the ingredients (except the ham) into a large mixing bowl and combine together.

2. Place the smoked ham on a roasting pan with the fat side up then generously coat with the mayonnaise mixture.

3. Add 1/2 cup of water into the roasting pan the transfer into an oven and bake for 15 minutes at 300°F.

4. Serve and enjoy with any side of your choice.

Nutrition Information

Calories: 486kcal | Fat: 46.9g | Carbohydrates: 8.4g | Protein: 9.7g

Slow Cooked BBQ Ribs

Preparation Time: 10 minutes

Cook Time: 8 hours 10 minutes

Servings: 3

Ingredients

1.1kg spare rib rack

for the bbq sauce

1/4 teaspoon stevia powder

1/2 cup crushed tomatoes

1/2 teaspoon cayenne pepper

1 tablespoon liquid smoke

1 tablespoon smoked paprika

1 tablespoon Worcestershire sauce

2 minced garlic cloves

salt & black pepper, to taste

Instructions

1. Using a small mixing bowl, add in all the bbq sauce ingredients and combine together.

2. Add the rib rack into a crock pot then coat with the bbq sauce mixture.

3. Cook for 8 hours on low settings or 4 hours on high settings.

Heat the oven up to 410°F then take the cooked ribs out of the pot and place on a baking tray.

4. Coat the tenderized rib rack with half of the remaining sauce in the crock pot until covered.

5. Place the baking tray in the oven and bake until the skin is crispy for 10 minutes.

6. Chop the baked ribs into sizes of choice then serve using the remaining bbq sauce in the pot as dip and enjoy.

Nutrition Information

Calories 804kcal | Fat: 62.94g | Carbohydrates: 4.33g | Protein 46.37g

Cheesy Red Pepper Bites

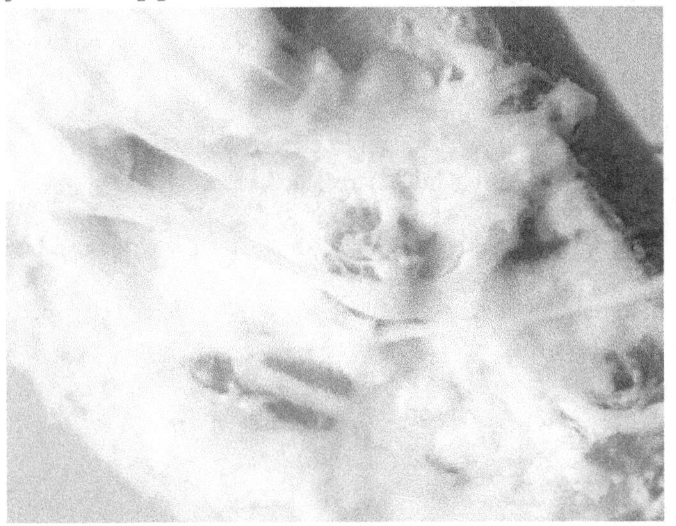

Preparation Time: 15 minutes

Cook Time: 20 minutes

Serving: 1

Ingredients

1/2 cup mayonnaise

1/2 teaspoon celery salt

1 teaspoon Dijon mustard

1 teaspoon cayenne pepper

1 teaspoon smoked paprika

1 cup roasted & chopped red peppers

2 cups shredded cheddar cheese

2 cups shredded extra-sharp cheddar cheese

Instructions

1. Place the chopped peppers face down on a baking sheet lined with parchment paper.

2. Heat the oven up to 450°F then place the baking sheet into the oven and bake for 20 minutes until lightly charred and wrinkly.

3. Once baked, peel off the skins and dispose of then chop into bites.

4. Add the remaining ingredients (except the salt) into the chopped pepper bites and combine together.

5. Add in the salt as desired and toss around again to combine.

6. Serve and enjoy.

Nutrition Information

Calories: 1156kcal | Fat: 103.7g | Carbohydrates: 8.6g | Protein: 43.2g

Cajun Blackened Fillets

Preparation Time: 5 minutes

Cook Time: 10 minutes

Servings: 4

Ingredients

1 lime juice

2 tablespoons vegetable oil

2 tablespoons Cajun blackening seasoning

4 (4 ounce) catfish fillets

Instructions

1. Generously coat the catfish with the Cajun seasoning until covered.

2. Pour the oil into a large skillet then heat up over medium high heat

3. Once hot, add in the catfish and cook for 5 minutes then flip over and cook for 5 more minutes.

4. Serve with a drizzle of the lime juice and enjoy.

Nutrition Information

Calories: 317kcal | Fat: 23g | Carbohydrates: 14.6g | Protein: 16g

Simple Crab Bisque

Preparation Time: 10 minutes

Cook Time: 15 minutes

Servings: 8

Ingredients

1/8 teaspoon cayenne pepper

1/4 teaspoon white pepper

1/4 cup sherry, if desired

1/2 teaspoon salt

1 diced small onion

1-pound lump crab meat

1 chopped red bell pepper

1 tablespoon vegetable oil

2 cups coconut milk

3 minced garlic cloves

3 cups vegetable stock

Instructions

1. Using medium sized pot pour in the vegetable oil and heat until hot.

2. Add in the garlic, onion and sauté until the onions translucent.

3. Add in bell peppers and sauté for 2 minutes then pour in the spices (except the salt).

4. Pour the coconut milk into the pot and simmer for 3 minutes.

5. Pour in the vegetable stock and simmer on low heat then add in the crab meat, sherry and heat through until the meat is cooked.

6. Serve and enjoy as desired.

Nutrition Information

Calories: 158kcal | Fat: 11g | Carbohydrate: 4g | Protein: 11g

Simple Coleslaw

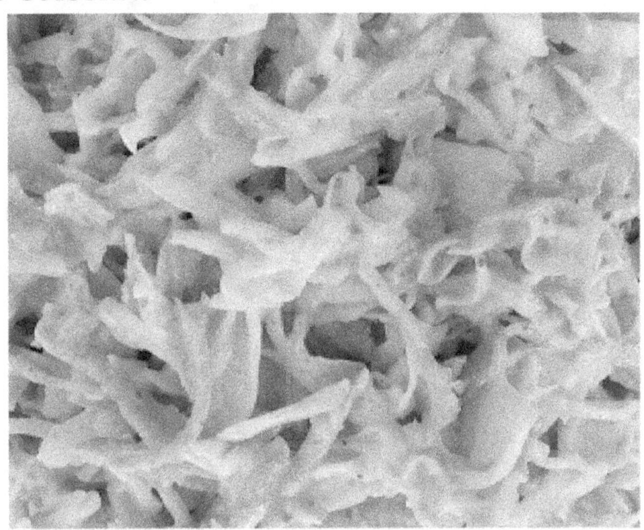

Preparation Time: 15 minutes

Cook Time: 0 minute

Servings: 6

Ingredients

1/4 teaspoon ground mustard

1/2 cup mayonnaise

1/2 cup diced carrots

1 1/2 tablespoons raw honey

1 tablespoon chopped parsley

1 cup thinly sliced red cabbage

2 tablespoons Apple cider vinegar

5 cup thinly sliced green cabbage

sea salt, to taste

Instructions

1. Using a large mixing bowl, add in the mustard, honey, vinegar, mayonnaise and whisk together until smooth and combined.

2. Season the mixture with salt & pepper as desired then add in the parsley, carrots, red & green cabbages and toss until coated with the mustard mixture.

3. Serve and enjoy.

Nutrition Information

Calories: 168kcal | Fat: 13.9g | Carbohydrate: 10.4g | Protein: 1.5g

Hot Sausage Gravy

Preparation Time: 5 minutes

Cook Time: 15 minutes

Servings: 8

Ingredients

1/8 teaspoon red pepper flakes

1/2 teaspoon xanthan gum

1 tablespoon sage leaves

1 cup low salt chicken stock

1-pound ground breakfast sausage

2 cups heavy cream

sea salt & black pepper, to taste

Instructions

1. Place a large skillet over medium high heat and heat until hot.

2. Add the sausage into the hot skillet, breaking into small chunks with a wooden spoon.

3. Brown the sausage over medium high heat until cooked through then drain off excess fat.

4. Reduce the heat to a medium low then top the browned sausage with the xanthan gum and stir together.

5. Add in the pepper flakes, sage and stir together then pour in the stock in bits.

6. Increase the heat to a medium and simmer the entire mixture until thick and gravy like.

7. Pour in the heavy cream, stir and simmer, occasionally stirring.

8. Reduce the heat and continue to simmer until thick as desired.

9. Season with the salt and pepper, taste, serve and enjoy.

Nutrition Information

Calories: 396kcal | Fat: 38g | Carbohydrates: 3g | Protein: 12g

Simple Mayo Deviled Eggs

Preparation Time: 7 minutes

Cook Time: 15 minutes

Servings: 12

Ingredients

1/8 teaspoon pepper

1/4 teaspoon salt

1/2 teaspoon dry mustard

5 tablespoons mayonnaise

6 hard-cooked eggs

paprika, to top

Instructions

1. Vertically half the eggs then scoop out the yolks and smash with a fork.

2. Add the pepper, mustard and salt into the smashed yolks and mix together.

3. Add the mayonnaise in bits and incorporate until a desired consistency is achieved.

4. Fill the empty egg whites with the yolk mixture until heaping then top with the paprika.

5. Serve and enjoy.

Nutrition Information

Calories: 81kcal | Fat: 6.9g | Carbohydrates: 0.4g | Protein: 3.1g

Nutty Cheese & Bacon Ball

Preparation Time: 30 minutes

Cook Time: 0 minute

Servings: 12

Ingredients

1/4 cup grated blue cheese

1/4 cup diced green onions

1/4 cup chopped fresh parsley

1/2 cup milk

3/4 cup divided pecans

1 tablespoon poppy seeds

1 jar diced & drained pimento

2 cups shredded sharp cheddar cheese

8 ounces' pack softened cream cheese

10 cooked & crumbled bacon slices

salt & black pepper, to taste

Instructions

1. Using a small mixing bowl, add in the cream cheese the mix with an electric hand mixer until well blended.

2. Add in the pimentos, onions, 1/2 of the pecans & bacon slices, remaining cheeses and beat again until incorporated.

3. Season with salt & pepper to taste then use a plastic wrap to mold the batter into ball and tightly wrap together.

4. Refrigerate the cheese ball for 2 hours until firm.

5. Using a large mixing bowl, add in the poppy seeds, parsley, remaining pecans and bacon and combine together.

6. Run the refrigerated cheese balls through the bacon pecans mix until properly coated.

7. Serve and enjoy or wrap and refrigerate until needed.

Nutrition Information

Calories: 204kcal | Fat: 16.6g | Carbohydrates: 3.9g | Protein: 10.5g

Lettuce Wrapped Bacon Bake

Preparation Time: 15 minutes

Cook Time: 30 minutes

Servings: 4

Ingredients

for the lettuce wraps

1 butter lettuce head

1 diced avocado, if desired

1 cup halved cherry tomatoes

8 chopped bacon slices

for the dressing

1/8 teaspoon powdered onion

1/8 teaspoon powdered garlic

1/4 cup almond milk

1 batch mayonnaise

1 teaspoon chopped dill

1 tablespoon juiced lime

1 tablespoon chopped chives

1 tablespoon chopped parsley

salt & pepper, to taste

Instructions

1. Prepare a baking sheet with a large parchment paper then arrange the bacon slices in a single layer on the sheet.

2. Heat the oven up to 425°F then place in the baking sheet and bake until golden brown and crispy for 30 minutes.

3. Transfer the baked bacon onto kitchen towels to drain off.

4. Using a large mixing bowl, add in the almond milk, powdered garlic & onion, chives, salt, pepper, dill, parsley, lime juice, mayonnaise and combine together.

5. Arrange the drained bacon slices on the butter lettuce wraps then garnish with the diced avocado, tomatoes and drizzle with the ranch dressing mixture.

6. Serve and enjoy as desired.

Nutrition Information

Calories: 422kcal | Fat 26.9g | Carbohydrate 6.4g | Protein 9g

END

Thank you for reading my book.

Janet Rooks